Why Is Snot Green?

And Other Extremely Important Questions (and Answers)

Glenn Murphy

Rb
Flash
Point

Roaring Brook Press
New York

Text copyright © 2007 by Glenn Murphy
Interior illustrations copyright © 2007 by Mike Phillips
Cover and "talking head" illustrations copyright © 2009 by Andy Rash

First published in the United Kingdom by Macmillan Children's Books,
a division of Macmillan Publishers Limited.
Flash Point is an imprint of Roaring Brook Press, a division of
Holtzbrinck Publishing Holdings Limited Partnership.
175 Fifth Avenue, New York, NY 10010

Cataloging-in-Publication Data is on file at the Library of Congress

Distributed in Canada by H. B. Fenn and Company, Ltd.
Roaring Brook Press books are available for special promotions and premiums.
For details contact: Director of Special Markets, Holtzbrinck Publishers.

Printed in March 2009 in the United States of America
by RR Donnelley, Harrisonburg, Virginia
First American Edition April 2009
1 3 5 7 9 10 8 6 4 2

Contents

This book is dedicated to
Heather and the Fuzzball.

Thanks to:
Damon and Gaby, for encouraging me to write
this in the first place
Karen, for giving me the time off to do it!
Everyone at the Science Museum who offered his or
her support, encouragement, and comments
Roger (glad I made you miss a few Tube stops, mate)
The Mitcham Massive (cheers, innit)
The Witts and the Murphs. Big love to you all.

Introduction

This is a book about science, and it's a book about answers. The answers to so many of those crazy questions you may have once thought about ... but then never quite got around to asking. And that's what science is all about: unanswered questions.

Too often, people don't read about science because they think it's too hard to understand, or just too boring to bother with. "Besides," they say, "science doesn't have all the answers."

They're right. It doesn't.

But it does, I think, have some of the very best questions.

"What is space made of?"

"Do spiders have ears?"

"What do people taste like to sharks and tigers?"

"Will evil robots take over the world one day?"

At the Science Museum in London, children and adults ask us questions like these every day. If we know, we'll try to answer, or help people to figure it out for themselves. Yet very often the answer just leads to another question. "But why is that?" they say. "How do you know that?" is another favorite. This leads to more explanations and even more questions. And that's how science works—we keep asking questions.

The main reason why science is such a useful way of thinking about things is that we're never happy just to say "I don't know" and leave it at that.

If we don't know, we *want* to know—and we'll keep on asking questions until we find out.

So, if you think science is too hard or too boring—you've just been asking the wrong questions. Now let's have some fun with some of the good ones.

Lost in Space

The universe can be a pretty dizzying place.

It was born in an almighty explosion of energy. It's so massively, hugely, immensely enormous that it's almost impossible to imagine how big it really is. Within it, there are spinning planets, burning suns, icy comets, and vast clouds of floating dust and rock. Planets, moons, and asteroids whip around each other like cosmic dance partners. Stars are born, stars die, and stars collapse into mysterious black holes in space.

But why did it turn out that way?

Where is it all headed?

Are we all alone in it?

And come on—how big could it really be?

Want to find out? Then read on . . .

How big is the universe?

Big. Really big. Crazy big. Billions of times bigger than the biggest thing you can imagine.

I don't know about that—I can imagine some pretty big stuff...

OK, let's give it a shot. Let's imagine the size of the universe. It's probably best to start small and work up—so let's start with something fairly big—the Earth. The Earth is about 8,000 miles wide. If you drove a tunneling car straight through the middle,* you'd get to the other side in about $5\frac{1}{2}$ days, going nonstop at an average highway speed of 60 mph.

That doesn't sound so far.

Right—it's not. So let's try a longer journey. Say, from here to the Moon. The Moon doesn't go around us in perfect circles—it gets closer and farther away from us at different times of the month. But, on average, it's about 240,000 miles away. It would take about 168 days to get there in a 60-mph flying space car. Even with rocket propulsion, the *Apollo* astronauts took about three days to get there (and it was really crowded in their spacecraft).

Similarly, the journey from Earth to the Sun is about 93

---

* You can't, of course—see *Could you dig your way through the Earth to China?* (page 55) if you're not sure why. But imagining this helps us get our heads around even bigger scales.

million miles, so it would take about 176 years by space car. To get right across our galaxy, the Milky Way, it would take about a million billion years (or 1,181,401,000,000,000 years to be more precise) to make the journey of 621 million billion (or 621,000,000,000,000,000) miles.

So what does that tell us?

That a space car would be cool, but at 60 mph it'd be pretty useless for getting around in space?

Errr... yes.

That, and that the galaxy is pretty huge in itself—let alone the universe. I'm running out of space to put all the zeros after the numbers here.

All right—what if you had a space car that could go at the speed of light?

Now we're talking. The speed of light is about 670 million mph, so a car that fast could go about 6 thousand billion miles (or 6 trillion miles) if it kept driving, nonstop, for a whole year. We call this distance a *light-year*, and it's much more useful for measuring the huge distances—between stars and

across galaxies—that we've been talking about. For example, the Milky Way is about 100,000 light-years across, so it'd take 100,000 years for our souped-up, super-fast, light-speed car to cross it. Still way too long to manage, but easier to imagine, maybe.

Go on, then—how big is the whole universe?

Well, we can only measure the universe as far as we can see it. With the best telescopes we have, that's about 15 billion light-years (or 90 billion trillion miles—I won't even bother trying to write that out with zeros) in every direction. So at the speed of light, it'd take at least 30 billion years to cross it. That's about 16 billion years longer than the age of the universe itself.

Ah. So it's big, then?

Like I said, *crazy* big. And that's just the part we can see. Beyond that, we know it extends even farther because the light from the stuff we can see at the "edge" has taken 14 billion years to reach us, and the universe has expanded quite a bit since then! It might even curve back on itself, like the sea does as you sail around the globe. If that were the case, you could circle the universe and end up back where you started.

Now that would be cool.

Yes, it would. But all your friends would be billions of years older. So even if they were still around, they probably wouldn't know what cool was any more. Bummer.

What is space made of?

Well, it's not just "nothing." Space is, at the very least, filled with gases spread out very, very thinly. It also bends—and possibly rips—so it must be made of something...

But space is, well, *space*, isn't it? No air, no gravity, ...

Well, not exactly. Gravity is actually everywhere in space.

Its pull becomes weaker the farther you move away from one particular source—like a planet—but it's still there.

And while it *is* true that there's no air in space, there are other things spread around it. It's only because the stuff is spread out so thin, and space is so big, that we can't detect it very easily.

So what is this "stuff"?

Mostly hydrogen and interstellar dust left over from the Big Bang.

How much of it is out there?

Well, there're billions of tons of it, but it's spread so far and wide across the universe that you won't find more than one atom per half a cubic inch of space in most places.*

* See *How big is the universe?* (page 4) to get a better idea of just how big that is.

You've probably been told that gases spread out to fill their containers, right? Well, if there's nothing else in the container, then they do. In this case, the container—the universe—was empty and is now at least 180 billion trillion miles wide. Spread over this distance, even billions of tons of material can look like virtually nothing. It just depends on how hard you're looking for it.

OK . . . so rather than say "there's nothing in space," you could say "there's _almost_ nothing in space" instead?
Exactly. That will not only be more accurate, but it will also freak people out. Which is always fun.

Top 10 things to do in Space

1   Float
2   Drift
3   Hover
4   Do somersaults
5   Spill some milk—and catch it again
6   Play zero-gravity football
7   Try to hit the Moon with a Frisbee
8   Draw a halo above your head with toothpaste
9   Wonder where your spaceship went
10 Panic

Why do planets bother going around the Sun?

Because the Sun's gravity pulls planets around it, preventing them from whizzing off into space. But despite this, the planets are still gradually inching away from the Sun over time.

Yikes. That doesn't sound good. I thought we'd just go around and around the Sun forever.
I'm afraid not. We're getting a tiny, tiny bit farther from the Sun with each lap we do around it. The Earth gets about a half inch farther away from the Sun every year.

Why's that?
It all has to do with how gravity works. A very clever scientist named Isaac Newton explained how gravity works over 300 years ago. If, like me, you can't read Latin and math gives you a headache, it basically goes like this:

- Everything attracts everything else.
- The bigger the things are, the bigger the pull.
- The closer together the things are, the bigger the pull.
- The force that causes this attraction is called gravity.

Now, the Sun is by far the biggest object in the solar system, so it pulls everything else toward it. That includes planets, comets, asteroids—everything.

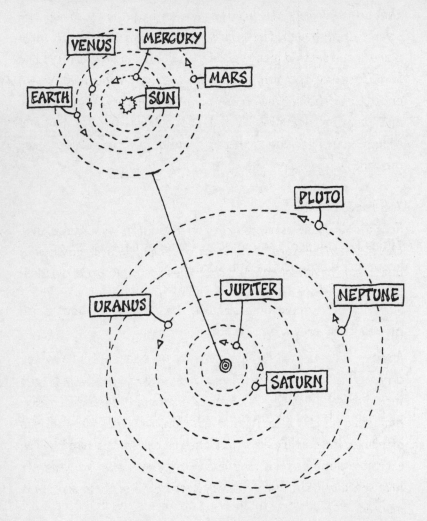

Hang on a minute—so why don't the planets all just get pulled right into the Sun?

That's because the planets all formed from chunks of stuff that were already circling the Sun to begin with. When the solar system began, these chunks clumped together to form planets and settled into regular circuits (or *orbits*) around the Sun. Closer to the Sun, all the icy bits got vaporized, so we ended up with the small rocky planets—Mercury, Venus, Earth, and Mars. Farther away, it was cool enough for gas to hang around, so we got the gas giant planets—Jupiter, Saturn, Uranus, and Neptune.

You forgot Pluto.

No, I didn't. Most astronomers don't count it as a real planet these days. There are a whole lot of small Pluto-sized objects out there beyond Neptune, and these (it has been decided) aren't planets either.

Oh.

Anyway—as I was saying—the planets have settled into more-or-less fixed orbits around the Sun. They don't get pulled right into it because they still have some circling speed (or rather, *momentum*)* left over from when they were just baby chunks of planet (or planetesimals, as they're called). It's like they're excitable puppies on a long leash—they're trying to whiz off into space but the Sun's gravity keeps pulling them around it instead.

---

* See *If the Earth spins around once a day, what started it spinning?* (page 24) for details.

So why are they gradually getting away from it, then?
Because the Sun is burning up its fuel and, in doing so, it's shrinking. As it gets smaller, the strength of its pull on the planets decreases.

Doesn't that mean we're going to fly off into space and freeze?
Well—do you want the good news or the bad news?

The bad . . .
Before any of this happens, the Sun will swell up into a red giant star and frazzle the Earth anyway.

Ouch. OK—the good . . .
It'll take a while, so there's a good chance we'll be able to hop planets (or preferably solar systems) beforehand.

Woohoo!! Better get cracking on those spaceships.
Yep. Time's awastin'—only got about 4.5 billion years left.

Why do stars twinkle?

Because we're looking at them through the murky veil of our atmosphere. From outside it, they look clear, steady, and bright.

You mean . . . stars don't twinkle? All those nursery rhymes—they lied to me!

Well, you could see it that way. The shifting brightness and shape that we see is actually caused by churning gases in our atmosphere, which we have to look through in order to see the stars. Outside the atmosphere, the light from the stars is more constant and even, so there's no "twinkle." From down here, though, they do seem to twinkle. So they weren't really lying. Whoever *they* are.

Fine. If they don't twinkle, what do they do?

They burn. They burn fiercely for billions of years. Then, when they die, some can explode with enough force to sweep up 1,000 suns—leaving nothing but a vast, deadly hole in space behind them.

OK, that sounds cooler than "twinkle." Tell me more.

Are you sitting comfortably? Good. Then let's begin . . .

Once upon a time there was a cool cloud of gas. It was pretty dense, but all its gas-cloud buddies thought it was cool, and everybody knew that one day it would become a star. There it was, minding its own business, doing whatever gas clouds do, until finally it collapsed. Under the pull of its own gravity, it crunched up on itself really tightly and got hotter and hotter, starting a chain reaction and turning the cloud into a huge, dangerous nuclear reactor floating in space.

This is my kind of nursery story . . .
Good, now there's a great bit coming up with giants and dwarfs in it, so be quiet.

Sorry.
No problem. Where was I? Ah, yes . . .

Well, by now the cloud had truly become a star. And it was enjoying itself immensely. It happily burned up its hydrogen gas—turning it into helium—for a few billion years, heating up a few nearby planets in the process. Life evolved on one or two planets, and the whole solar system bobbed along happily in its arm of the galaxy. Until one day the star had used up nearly all the hydrogen in its core and was forced to frazzle the nearby planets as it grew into a *red giant.*

As if that wasn't enough, its core shrank some more over the next few billion years. Then it became a giant again, then it shrank a bit again, until eventually the star had had enough and decided to go out in style. So it imploded.

The rebounding explosion—
a *supernova*—burned brighter
than the entire galaxy and
left behind a huge invisible
hole in space (a black hole),
from which nothing that fell
in could ever escape.

    The end.

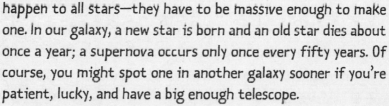

**Wow! That was excellent. Can I
see one of those now, please?**
Well, these supernova explosions don't
happen to all stars—they have to be massive enough to make
one. In our galaxy, a new star is born and an old star dies about
once a year; a supernova occurs only once every fifty years. Of
course, you might spot one in another galaxy sooner if you're
patient, lucky, and have a big enough telescope.

    Similarly, not all supernova explosions leave behind a black
hole. Plus, you can't see a black hole, unfortunately, as nothing
can escape from it—not even light.

Boo. Some happy ending . . .
There's no pleasing some people.

> ## Who's firing all the shooting stars?

> No one is. They're just small lumps of space dust plowing into our atmosphere and burning up. Besides—it's often *us* running into *them*.

Come again?

It's true. If you think about it, the Earth is going around the Sun—a round trip of about 584 million miles—once every 365 days. This means the Earth is traveling at about 67,000 miles per hour. Just imagine—you and I, and everyone else on the planet, are doing 67,000 mph right now.

Whoa. Why does it feel like I'm sitting still, then?

Because just like when you're on a fast (but comfy) train, you don't really notice you're moving until you look out the window to see the world whipping by in the other direction.

That's what happens when we see shooting stars—we see the evidence that we're moving through space. Rather rapidly too.

Huh? How did you get all that from a little streak in the sky?

Next time you're lucky enough to spot a shooting star, try and figure out which bit of the sky it came from and keep watching that spot. Chances are you'll see more of them—loads of shooting stars that seem to shoot up, down, to the left, and to the right of the same central point in the night sky. It's a bit like being directly underneath a shower head and looking up—you see droplets fanning out in every direction.

Cool—but what does that mean?

It means that the whole Earth is moving at 67,000 mph, and its path crosses chunks of rock and dust also moving through space. As each chunk slams into our atmosphere, it heats up due to friction, and most chunks burn up completely way before they hit the ground. This makes the burning streak in the sky that we call a *meteor,* or a shooting star. Chunks that burn for longer, we call fireballs. Chunks that make it to the ground, we call meteorites.*

Got it. But if we're always moving, and always hitting rocks and stuff, why don't we see meteor showers all the time?

Well, we do hit (or get hit by) bits of dust and rock millions of times every day and night. But these are random individual chunks (or meteoroids), and it's easy to miss their meteor trails in such a big sky if you don't know where to look.

Meteor *showers* happen when the Earth plows through a swarm of meteoroids in space—like those left behind by passing comets as bits break off them. When this happens, you get lots of meteors at once, and you can easily spot them one after another if you're looking in the right direction.

---

* See *Could comets or asteroids really blow up the Earth if they hit us—like in the movies?* (page 43) for other similar definitions, like meteoroids, asteroids, and comets.

But how would you know where to look?
Astronomers can often predict where the showers will be in
the sky because we pass through some of the same swarms
every year (at the same point in the Earth's circuit around the
Sun). So, if you want to, you can find out where and when, and
head out for an evening's meteor spotting.

Go on, give it a shot!

Know your stuff:
cool things to see by night

Meteor showers: Big ones happen every
year around the same date. These include the
Leonids (around November 17) and Perseids
(around August 12).

Lunar eclipses: These happen when the Moon
lies in the shadow of the Earth, causing it to
change color from white to a deep red. The next
few visible from North America are on June 26,
2010, December 21, 2010, and December 10,
2011.

Comets: These are a bit rarer. Although there
are many visible with telescopes, the next time
we see one just by looking up might not be
until Halley's Comet returns in 2061. But there's
always a chance a bright, shiny new one might
turn up—as Comet Hale-Bopp did in 1997.

What are Saturn's rings made of, and why don't other planets have them?

The rings of Saturn are made of millions of small chunks of ice the size of tennis balls. And other planets—including Neptune, Uranus, and Jupiter—actually have rings too.

Really? They have rings too? How come you never see them in pictures?

Saturn's rings are easier to see—they're pretty clear to anyone looking at the planet with a half-decent telescope. In fact, Galileo spotted what he called "ears" on Saturn with his telescope way back in the seventeenth century, but he couldn't explain them. Almost fifty years later, another physicist and astronomer, Christiaan Huygens, recognized them as rings around the planet. Saturn has been famous as "the ringed planet" ever since.

Even though they couldn't see them directly, astronomers in the 1970s predicted that Neptune and Uranus would have rings; they didn't get a clear picture of them until the *Voyager* satellite swung by them in the 1980s. On the way there, it spotted rings around Jupiter too—which was a nice surprise. So there *are* pictures of rings on other planets—it's just that fewer people have seen them.

Are all those rings made of ice too?

Some are ice, some are chunks of dust or rock, and some are probably a mix of all of these.

We know that Saturn's, Neptune's, and Uranus's rings are made of millions of small chunks of dirty ice—most of them smaller than a tennis ball. Jupiter's single ring seems to be made of tiny dust particles.

How did they get there, and why doesn't Earth have them?

Small planets and moons don't seem to have rings, so we think only big planets can have them. One idea is that they are formed when a moon gets too close to the planet it orbits. When this happens, tidal forces caused by the pull of the planet's gravity rip the moon apart. The pieces then spread out and encircle the planet, forming a ring that shows where the moon used to orbit. The Earth and the smaller planets aren't big enough to rip their moons apart, so they don't make rings.

So why are Saturn's rings the biggest and best, then?

Well, it's true that Saturn's rings are the most impressive. The pieces are so small, and there are so many of them, that together they look like a single big icy disk. It could be that Saturn used to have a big, icy moon that was smashed into tiny bits when it was hit by a comet or an asteroid. That'd do it.

I like that. That's *definitely* what happened.

It's as good a guess as any.

> If the Earth's a big ball, why don't we fall off the bottom of it?

> Because Earth's gravity doesn't make things fall down—it makes things fall toward the middle of the planet. That goes for everything on Earth—its skies, its oceans, and its people.

Oh, yeah. Of course. Er . . . what?
Let's go back a bit. Isaac Newton told us how gravity works—like how and why things fall toward the ground when you drop them, and how fast you can expect them to go when you do. Agreed?

S'pose so.
OK. Well, he also told us that gravity wasn't just about things falling toward the ground, but rather all objects falling toward—or attracting—each other. This force of attraction is stronger for larger objects, and Earth is by far the largest object on . . . well . . . Earth. So everything on Earth is held on by the Earth's super-strong gravity. Like a big ball-shaped magnet with bits stuck all over it—not just metals, but all kinds of things, like air, water, trees, and people. That's why none of it falls off.

OK—I get that. But magnets work by being *magnetic*, right? So why does gravity work just because something is big?

Good question. You're right—there is a bit of the story missing here. So here's the rest . . .

Newton's explanation of gravity was all very clever—and we've since used it to figure out everything from orbiting planets to moon landings—but he still didn't say what gravity actually *is*.

Where did the force come from? Why was it there at all? Newton didn't know, couldn't say.

So Albert Einstein bravely had a crack at these and other questions almost two hundred years later, saying (more or less):

- Space is not empty, or even flat—it's more like a fabric with lumps and dents in it.
- The lumps and dents are distortions caused by objects (like stars and planets) in the fabric.
- Gravity is just objects rolling into dents (or around lumps) in the fabric.

Er . . . having trouble with this one . . .

OK—try to picture it like this: Imagine space as a big sheet of rubber, and the Sun as a basketball plunked in the middle. The sheet will bend around the ball, making a big dent in it, right? Now imagine rolling a few marbles or tennis balls across the sheet: Some will go straight across, but the ones that pass close to the basketball will get drawn into an arc around it as they dip into the dent. The marbles might even do a complete circle around the basketball before contacting it.

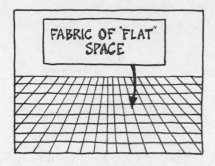

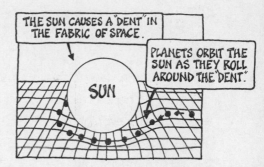

So...

So this is why planets circle (or orbit) the Sun—not just planets, but asteroids and comets too. It's also the reason why moons orbit planets, and why satellites and space shuttles can orbit the Earth.

Basically, big things make a dent in space, and other things "roll" or "fall" toward the source of the dent. If they have enough speed and momentum, small things can circle around and around the dent forever. If they don't have enough speed, they fall into the dent and eventually settle next to the object that made it.

So planets, comets, and asteroids roll around a gravity dent made by the Sun. The Moon rolls around one made by the Earth. Rockets and satellites get launched to the edge of the gravity dent and roll around it until it's time to come back.

And the skies, oceans, deserts, glaciers, trees, animals, and people of Earth all sit in the depths of a dent in space created by the planet—stuck to its surface by the force of gravity.

Dents in space, eh? Weird.

You said it.

If the Earth spins around once a day, what started it spinning?

The Sun and planets were formed when bits of a huge spinning dust cloud clumped together to form solid lumps. The Earth—like all the other clumps—has kept on spinning ever since.

Let me get this straight—the whole solar system was born from a lump of spinning space dust?

Basically, yes. All stars and planets are born this way. Get enough dust in one place at one time, and gravity will start pulling things together. When enough dust accumulates, it collapses in on itself, heats up, and forms a star. If the dust was rotating beforehand, the star will rotate too and draw other lumps of dust into circuits around it. These circling dust lumps become planets, and the star becomes a sun. The sun and the dust lumps around it continue to spin long after they have formed.

But wouldn't they slow down after a while? Most spinning things slow down and stop in the end, don't they?

That's true—most things we see every day do stop spinning in the end. But, when they do, they don't just stop all by themselves—there's a force that's working against the spin and slowing them down. That force is friction.

Let's say you're spinning a coin on a table. From the second you release it, it's constantly being slowed down as it whips against the air around it and scratches against the table below. If you spun that coin while floating in space, however, it would keep spinning forever. There would be no air (or table surface) to rub against, and so no friction to slow it down.

This is what happens with spinning suns and planets. In fact, they even speed up a bit as they are formed.

Huh? How's that? I don't get that at all.

As the spinning sun or planet clumps together, it gets denser but also smaller in size. When this happens, its speed of rotation increases because it's now moving in a tighter circle. You see this happen when Olympic ice skaters do a spin: They start by spinning slowly with their arms wide apart, then pull them in to go faster. Same thing with stars, planets, and space dust.

OK—I get it. So the Earth clumped up, shrank up, and sped up until it was spinning around once a day?

Not quite. It sped up at first, but then slowed down. In fact, its spin is still slowing down now. Spinning planets and stars can be slowed down a bit by each other's gravity. We call these effects *tidal forces*. In fact, the Moon has been applying a constant tidal force on the Earth (and the Earth upon the Moon too) for billions of years now, and this has slowed the spin of the Earth by quite a bit. Thanks to that, the days and nights are getting longer and longer.

Cool! So every day I get to sleep in longer and have more time to see my friends?
Well . . . a *bit* longer. It's only getting longer by about two milliseconds (or thousandths of a second) every century at the moment. Not much of a sleep-in, really.

I can't wait. Ha-ha!! Just think—in a few billion years I might get an extra hour in bed . . .
Er . . . OK. If you say so.

Will the Sun go out one day?

Yes, like all stars, the Sun will one day shine no more—ending its life as a ball of white ash. But by then we'll be fried, rather than frozen.

But if the Sun goes out, won't we all freeze?
If it just fizzled out like a sparkler on the Fourth of July, then yes, we would. But that's not how stars die. Depending on how big they are, lots of things can happen to stars before they finally kick the bucket. As for our Sun, it'll swell up into a monstrous red giant; barbecue Mercury, Venus, and the Earth . . . and eat them.

Harsh! Why would it do that?!

It doesn't have a choice. Once most of the hydrogen gas is converted to helium, the inside of it will collapse, and the hydrogen burning on the outside will be pushed outward. As it does this, it'll grow much bigger—big enough to swallow Mercury, Venus, and maybe Earth too.

Should we move to Mars now, then?

Not just yet. We'll be fine for the time being. Most stars like the Sun live for about 10 billion years, and ours has only been around for about 5 billion—so it's roughly middle aged. It'll be at least 4.5 billion years before it turns into a red giant, and a few billion more before it finally collapses and ends its life as a burned-out white dwarf.

Whew. That's a relief.

On the other hand, life on Earth will have had it long before the Sun engulfs the planet.

What?!

And even if you make it to Mars, it won't be very comfortable for anything to live there either.

Hey—no fair! Why not?

Because most of life as we know it can survive only when the temperature is just right. Some animals can survive in the desert at temperatures of over 248°F, but even they couldn't stand it much hotter. Turn the temperature up by an average of 50° or 70°F, and you'd kill most things on the planet. Things in the sea would survive a bit longer, but even they would keel over once the oceans had boiled and evaporated. Again, all this would happen way before the Sun engulfed the planet itself.

Will it happen all at once, or will we see it coming?

It'll take a while, and (if we're all still here in 4.5 billion years) we'll know when it's about to happen—the Sun will turn red as the hydrogen inside it moves to the surface. Don't panic and confuse this with a normal sunset, though.

Is there nothing we can do to protect ourselves?

Sunscreen, maybe. If you can find some with an SPF of 5,000.

That's not funny.

Sorry.

Know your stuff: types of star

Yellow dwarf: Young and fairly small. Our Sun is a yellow dwarf star.

Red dwarf: The most common type. Relatively small, cool, and faint. Proxima Centauri is a nearby one.

Red giant: Older, bigger, and hotter. Betelgeuse, 600 light-years away from us, is one of these. It's 20 times bigger and 14,000 times hotter than our Sun.

Supergiant: The biggest stars. When they die, they explode (supernova), and some become black holes.

White dwarf: Small and very dense.

Neutron star: Incredibly small and dense. Some are less than 10 miles wide, but weigh more than the Earth.

Pulsar: A spinning neutron star that emits pulses of energy. Often mistaken for alien radio signals.

Binary star: Two stars circling each other. About half of all stars in the sky are actually pairs of stars like this.

Pop star: Loud, rich, annoying. Likes to sing.

Gangsta: Tough, moody. Shines with a "bling."

Where did the Moon come from?

Our best guess is that the Moon came from the Earth. Astronomers think that a massive asteroid hit us billions of years ago—blasting huge chunks of molten rock out of the planet and into orbit. The Moon formed from the shrapnel.

That may well be the coolest thing I have ever heard. The Moon formed because we were hit by a space missile?

Yes. Well, sort of. But it was probably more like a violent trick-shot in a game of cosmic pool. The asteroid was huge—probably about the same size as Mars—and it struck the Earth a glancing edgeways blow. The chunks of rock released in the impact were so hot that they actually vaporized. It was only later that these bits clumped up and reformed into molten—and then solid—rock.

Is this how all moons get made? By asteroids hitting planets?

Some moons are made this way, but probably not many. Asteroid impacts are fairly common—especially on bigger planets like Jupiter and Saturn because they're bigger targets. But they have to be pretty big asteroids to throw debris out into space—most just leave a hole and a heap of rocks around it, which we see as a crater.

By big asteroids hitting planets, then?

Well, even if it is a big enough impact, more often than not any rocky debris released from an explosion is thrown right out into space and lost forever. In fact, most of the vaporized rock released from the Earth's big impact was lost in this way—only some of it was held in orbit by the Earth's gravity and clumped together to form the Moon.

Also, just because some debris gets captured doesn't mean it'll automatically shape itself into a nice, round moon. Sometimes the bits just encircle the planet, and you get rings instead. Sometimes you get moons and rings—as seen on Saturn. There, several small "shepherd" moons orbit alongside the rings, helping to hold their shape.

So where do all the other moons come from?

Some form around the same time as (or just after) their host planets, from bits drawn in by the new planet's gravity. Others are "captured" by a planet's gravity much later on. Big planets like Jupiter and Saturn have collected many of their moons (between them, they have more than 30!) in this way.

Could that happen here, giving us an extra moon?

Yes, it could. And it may have happened already.

Huh? We have two moons?

Kind of. About twenty years ago, astronomers spotted an object about 2 miles wide, not that far from Earth, and named it Cruithne. About ten years ago, they realized that it was still with us—sharing our orbit around the Sun—and that it is actually orbiting the Earth. But while the Moon takes just a month to do this, Cruithne takes about 770 years, and it will eventually leave us, flinging away into space forever. So you could say it's a Near-Earth Asteroid (NEA) with temporary moon status.

But if a planet has lots of moons, don't they all crash into each other?

Not at all. When planets have more than one moon, the moons are usually all different sizes, so they orbit at different distances. Even when they're the same size, they can settle into a shared orbit like Saturn's moons Janus and Epimethius and just chase each other around the planet like a pair of happy cosmic puppies.

One last thing: If the Moon came from the Earth, does that mean the Moon's made of the same stuff?

Yes, but in different amounts. Both have a crust of solid rock floating on top of a mantle of semimolten rock.* Both also have a core of iron and nickel in the middle. But inside, the Moon is much cooler than the Earth, so while the Earth has a solid inner core and a liquid outer core, the Moon's outer core is still pretty solid. A bit gloppy, at best.

No cheese, then?

Sadly, no.

---

* See *Why don't earthquakes happen everywhere at once?* (page 58) for a better understanding of what the Earth is made of, and how it all fits together.

Do UFOs exist, and could my math teacher be an alien?

UFOs definitely exist—they're spotted all the time. But none yet have been alien spacecraft. And your math teacher is probably just a (weird) human— no matter how alien he seems.

Hang on a minute—you said UFOs *do* exist?
Yes. Definitely. They're spotted all the time, all over the world.

Aha! Got you! So there are flying saucers, then! You're just covering it up, like all the shifty science guys on *The X-Files*...
No, I'm not.

Yeah, right—you *would* say that. You're one of them.
Listen—*UFO* just means "unidentified flying object," right? That basically means anything in the sky not clearly identified as something sensible like an airplane, glider, helicopter, balloon, or bird.

La, la, la... I'm not li-sten-ing... you're just trying to brainwash me with your evil government conspiracy stuff... la, la, la...
So—look, stop it, I'm not brainwashing you—that means even

a tennis ball or a Frisbee can be a UFO, at least temporarily (or until someone says, "Hey, wait a minute—that's just a Frisbee!").

Yeah, whatever. Some of them are huge, and they glow in the dark. So if they're not spaceships, then what are they?

Some are just the result of rare atmospheric events, like *sprites* and *ball lightning*. Scientists still aren't completely sure exactly how they are formed, because it's not like you can study them "in the wild." But it's thought that they happen when lightning strips bits off nitrogen atoms in the air, leaving a glowing ball of colored plasma (or super-heated gas) behind.

Sprites form in the upper atmosphere, about 13 miles above the ground. Each one lasts less than a second, but when lots of them appear and disappear in a row, they can look like a single, fast-moving object.

Ball lightning can appear nearer to the ground, creating an eerie glowing ball (sometimes with a tail). This can hover and float about for several seconds before disappearing or discharging itself into a nearby object.

What about the UFOs that last longer than a few seconds?
Some sightings have turned out to be unusual but real military aircraft. Their existence may be denied at the time to keep them secret, but we find out later what they are (think

how strange a stealth bomber would have looked thirty years ago). Others are just hoaxes, ranging from the very good (using Hollywood-style digital effects) to the very poor (the Frisbee-on-a-string-dangled-in-front-of-a-video-recorder type).

What about those alien crop circles?

A clever but proven hoax, created by two guys with planks and ropes. They even owned up to it and showed how it was done.

But what about aliens kidnapping people?

Well, many have been reported, but look at it this way: almost all of them have been in the United States, the UK, and France. These three countries make up only 6% of the world's land mass. So either aliens are ignoring the other 94% of the world (and the entire Southern Hemisphere) . . . or we're ignoring the evidence.

In the United States alone, over 5 million people have claimed they were abducted over the last fifty years. That's 2,470 a day. You'd think maybe someone would notice all that flying-saucer traffic . . .

So aliens aren't real, then?

I didn't say that. There could well be aliens out there—it's just that we almost certainly haven't met any of them yet. If you're looking for evidence, you can join the Search for Extraterrestrial Intelligence (SETI)* project. They haven't found any aliens yet either, but they have a better chance of finding real ones than anyone else on the Internet.

* www.seti.org

. . . and my math teacher isn't one?
Probably not. I can't say for sure, but I'm betting he's more inhuman than nonhuman. Mine was, at least. Better do what he says, just in case . . .

What would happen if you farted in a space suit?

It would be the worst kind of fart ever: You couldn't deny it, you couldn't escape it, and the smell would stay with you all the way back to the space station.

Couldn't you just open a flap or something and let it out?
You mean open the suit? Ummm . . . no. You wouldn't want to do that.

Why's that? Would you suffocate?
Well, no—not necessarily. In many space suits, the oxygen supply is sealed off in the helmet, so you'd still be able to breathe even if you opened a flap somewhere else.

So why not just pop open a handy bum-flap, then?
Bad idea. Trust me on this.

But why?

OK, you asked for it . . .

For an astronaut in space, the suit
is all that stands between you and
the deadly airless vacuum outside. Open
a flap in your suit to let the fart out, and
the air in your lungs and guts would expand,
causing them to swell and rupture if it happened quickly enough. Then water in the muscles and soft tissues would boil into an expanding vapor, bloating parts of your body to up to twice their
normal size. Then bubbles of nitrogen gas would form in your
blood vessels, causing immense pain as they pressed on the
nerves around them. And—eventually—you'd freeze.

Ooh, that's gotta hurt. But why would that happen? And how could you boil and freeze at the same time?

This is all due to one thing: In space there's no atmosphere
around you—so there's nothing to keep your body under pressure, and nothing to absorb and retain heat.

I don't get it.

OK, let me explain. On Earth, the atmosphere is constantly
pushing against your body. Without it, the air in your lungs
and guts would push outwards unopposed, and the water in
your soft tissues would start to boil. This is because there
are two ways of boiling liquids: One is to heat them up, breaking the weak bonds between the molecules inside. The other
is to drop the pressure around the liquid, taking away the

squashing force that keeps the molecules packed tightly together. This allows them to drift apart, and the liquid turns into a gas.

The temperature of the water in your body tissues is normally kept at about 98.6°F and is happily kept liquid under the pressure of the atmosphere. But in space there is no atmosphere, so 98.6°F is enough to boil some of your body fluids.

A space suit stops this from happening by keeping the body under constant pressure. It does this by inflating on the inside (like a bike tire) and constantly pressing against the skin. But if you released this pressure—by, say, opening a handy bum-flap to let out a fart—the water in your tissues would boil and bubble. This would also make your skin and organs swell up as the blood inside them expanded.

Yuck. Nasty. OK, what about the freezing part?

This would follow the nasty lung-swelling part if you found yourself in the shade (for example, if the Earth, Moon, or your spacecraft is between you and the Sun). Without a thick atmosphere of gases to hold the heat, temperatures in shaded space reach well below −148°F. A space suit is lined with special insulating materials that stop you from losing the heat inside (produced by your body) to the outside. Open a flap in it and all the heat radiates out of your suit and into space, freezing you solid within minutes.

So, if you fart in a space suit, you're stuck with it?

I'm afraid so. Of course, some of it will be recycled into the suit's life-support system, so you'll breathe a lot of it back in.

Ugh!

The rest will drift out when you get back to the ship and take the suit off. No doubt making you very unpopular with the other astronauts, since you can't open a window in there either.

So no eating beans in space, then?

Not unless you want to be called Major Fartpants all the way home . . .

What is a black hole, and what would happen if you fell into one?

It's a super-massive object, left behind after the death of some stars, from which nothing—not even light—can escape. If you fell into one, you'd be ripped apart, fried, or trapped forever. Possibly all three.

Black holes are dead stars?

Yes, kind of. Although not all stars end up as black holes—some just burn out. Otherwise there would be black holes everywhere.

So how do you get one?

If a star is big enough—and we're talking at least twenty to twenty-five times bigger than the Sun here—it will end its fiery life in a massive explosion called a *supernova*. When this happens, the outer shell of the star gets blown apart, but its inner core collapses in on itself. For some, the core forms a small, dense lump, and the star ends its life there. For others, the core just keeps getting smaller and denser and smaller and denser. The pull of its gravity is so immense that anything within a certain distance gets sucked in and is trapped forever. Like a huge spherical invisible whirlpool in space.

Cool. But why are they invisible?

Because nothing within a certain distance of the black hole's center (a boundary line we call the *event horizon*) can get out of it—not even light. It was Albert Einstein who figured out, among other things, that light is actually bent around massive objects like stars by gravity. If the object is super-massive, like a black hole, then any light rays close enough to it will spiral right around into it and never escape its grasp. So it's not just that it fails to *make* light (as stars do)—you can't even see light bouncing off it (as we can with moons and planets). So it becomes invisible, and we can only perceive it as a "gap" in space. As you might imagine, these are not easy to spot!

So how do we know they're even there?

By looking for telltale signs of light bent around them—light that passes close enough to be affected by the black hole's gravity, but not so close that it gets sucked into it. Once you spot that, you can confirm the black hole is there by looking for X-rays. This is because things that are being sucked into the hole heat up as they spin around it, and when they get hot enough, they start to radiate X-rays. So if you spot a weird light-bending pattern in space and it's also emitting X-rays, there's a good chance it's a black hole.

So why would all that nasty stuff happen if you fell in one?

Well, you'd be ripped apart by tidal forces caused by its super-strong gravity. Basically, if you jumped in feet first, your feet and legs would be sucked in faster than your head and upper body (or vice versa if you dove in head first). So your body would be stretched out lengthwise until you snapped like a rubber band.

Ouch!

But let's say you fired yourself into the black hole from a super-fast cannon. Maybe you could go fast enough to get to the middle before this happened. Even so, the chances are all those X-rays it chucks out would fry you before you made it through.

Eeek! But what if you managed to survive that somehow? What would happen then?

Actually, no one knows for sure. We know you could never escape the black hole's gravity, so you'd never come out of it again. You could be trapped forever. But some scientists think it's possible that black holes are "wormholes" in space: doorways to other points in the universe, or even other universes. But if you think about it, even if you made it in alive, it's not clear how you'd escape the door on the other side, since this would be a black hole too.

Stretched, snapped, fried, and possibly trapped forever, eh? Remind me not to try that . . .

Absolutely. There are probably safer ways to travel!

> **Could comets or asteroids really blow up the Earth if they hit us—like in the movies?**

> They probably couldn't blow up the whole planet, but they could give it a good whack and wipe out everything living on it. And dodging them wouldn't be as easy as in the movies either . . .

What's the difference between an asteroid and a comet, anyway?

Well, they're basically similar: lumps of rock, dust, and ice in space. They're debris left over from the formation of the solar system—the spare bits that didn't get to be part of a star, planet, or moon. The main differences lie in where they come from and how they behave.

Where *do* they come from?

Asteroids form from small particles of dust and rock that pull together under their own gravity into lumps of various sizes. They can be anything from 30 feet to about 620 miles wide. In our solar system, most of them orbit the Sun in a huge ring or asteroid belt between Mars and Jupiter. There, Jupiter's gravity holds them in place, keeps them spread out, and stops them from forming bigger lumps (like a moon or even a small planet). But sometimes one of them will get knocked or pulled out of orbit, and when this happens, they can end up on collision courses with planets.

Comets are formed far from the Sun and have a core (or coma) made of dust and ice surrounded by a crust of dust and rock. Most of them begin life in belts or clouds way beyond the planets. From there, they're pulled inward by the Sun's gravity, and they start doing huge, oval-shaped laps around the Sun that can take hundreds or even thousands of years. Comets also melt as they pass close to the Sun, venting trails of rock, dust, and water vapor—which we see as the comet's "tail." Some comets end up spiraling inward and crash into the Sun. When this happens, we give them one of the coolest names in astronomy: sungrazers.

Have we ever been hit by one before?

It's not clear whether the Earth has ever been hit by a comet, but we've certainly been hit by a number of good-sized asteroids. These are a bit more commonplace. In fact, a decent-sized asteroid explodes in the upper atmosphere—with the force of a small nuclear weapon—more than once a year.

But thankfully, there haven't been any really big ones for a while now. The last really big one to hit us was in 1908, when an asteroid exploded above Tunguska, Siberia. This blew with the force of 1,000 atomic bombs, leaving no crater, but flattening more than 770 square miles of forest below. And that was nothing compared to the comet or asteroid that caused the 9,500-square-mile crater in Chicxulub, Mexico. That one hit us about 65 million years ago and is thought to have killed— among many other things—practically all of the dinosaurs.*

* See Why are there no dinosaurs any more? (page 131) for details.

What would happen if a big one hit us tomorrow?

Well, if the Chicxulub one is anything to go by, an asteroid about 6 miles across would punch right into the atmosphere as if it wasn't there. The explosion on impact would vaporize the asteroid, the ground, and just about anything else within a 60-mile radius, leaving a hole in the Earth about that wide. Some of the dust and rock thrown up by the blast would fly so high, it'd go into orbit around the Moon. The rest would rain back down on the planet like fire, cooking anything or anyone not hiding deep underground and enveloping the Earth in a dark, choking cloud. This would then block out the Sun for about a year, killing all plant life and most or all of the animal life along with it. So, even if you survived the blast, you'd probably starve to death.

Couldn't you just hide underground with a year's supply of ramen noodles or something?

Maybe. But even if ramen noodles were that nutritious (which they aren't), it's unlikely you could get enough for everyone.

Couldn't we just blow them up?

Sadly, no. Even Bruce Willis couldn't do it. All the bombs and missiles on the planet could barely dent a good-sized asteroid or comet. But we might be able to knock one off course by hitting it sideways. Some scientists think we could even attach a kind of solar sail to an asteroid in space so that the solar wind would push it off course gradually over time.

That's crazy!

Not as crazy as eating nothing but ramen noodles for a year.

Know your stuff: space rocks

Asteroid: Any one of the thousands of smallish (30 feet to 620 miles wide) rocky objects that orbit the Sun.

Asteroid belt: A ring of asteroids orbiting the Sun. The largest belt in our solar system lies between Jupiter and Mars.

Comet: An object made of dust, ice, and rock that melts as it nears the Sun, releasing gases seen as a long "tail" or trail across the night sky.

Meteor: A streak of light across the sky seen as a small object enters the Earth's atmosphere and burns up. A shooting star.

Meteorite: A small chunk of rock that has made it all the way to the ground, striking the surface of a planet or moon.

Meteoroid: A chunk of rocky matter, typically smaller than an asteroid. Causes a meteor as it burns up in the atmosphere.

Meteor shower: Lots of meteors spotted at once, which all seem to come from the same point in the sky.

Micrometeorite: A tiny meteorite. Millions of these hit the Earth each day.

What did the Big Bang sound like?

Like nothing at all—because
1. there was nobody there to hear it,
2. sound can't travel through space,
3. there was no space for it to travel through, and
4. there was no real bang anyway.

Whoa! Hold on, there. I think I get the first bit . . .
Right—the first bit's easy. The Big Bang—the huge eruption of matter and energy that started the expansion of the universe—happened about 13 billion years ago. That's a really, really long time ago.

To give you some idea of how long: Our planet, Earth, is only about $4\frac{1}{2}$ billion years old (that's 4,500,000,000 years). Life didn't appear on it until 3 billion years ago. The first humans didn't evolve until about 40,000 years ago. The ancient Egyptians, the Romans, and all that lot didn't hit the scene until about 3,000 years ago. So you could say we missed the Bang by quite a bit.

OK—but if we were there, what would it have sounded like?
Like nothing. Nada. Zip. Not a peep. Total silence.

Eh? Why not?

Because for you to hear a sound, it has to travel *from* something (like an alarm clock, or the barrel of a gun) *through* something (like air or water) and *into your ears*, where it wobbles your eardrums. Then your brain translates that wobbling into a sound (like *Brrrrrrrrrnnnggg!* or *Bang!*).

The problem with bangs in space is that even if you make one, the sound has nothing* to travel through, so it doesn't make it to your ears. (The same goes for exploding spaceships in science-fiction films—you wouldn't hear those either).

So, even if you were hovering right next to the Big Bang, listening for it, you wouldn't hear a thing.

Some scientists have pointed out that you can translate the radiation left over from the Big Bang into an audible sound using a computer. But even if you do that, it just sounds like a constant hissing sound, rather than a big impressive *Kablooie* or *Kaboom!*

But that's ridiculous. Why call it "the Big Bang," then?

Well, it was a big explosion, of a sort. It was an explosion of matter, energy, and space. It just didn't go *Bang!*

And besides—"The Big Explosion of Matter and Energy" isn't as catchy.

---

* Or almost nothing, anyway—see *What is space made of?* (page 7) for a detailed explanation.

OK, fine—you couldn't hear the Big Bang because you can't hear bangs in space. Got it.
Well . . . not quite. There's another problem. There was no space before the Big Bang either.

Er . . . come again? If there was no space, what was there?
Nothing. Absolutely nothing. The Big Bang didn't just create all the stars and planets floating in space—it created the space they were floating in too. Space isn't just nothingness—it's like a fabric that the galaxies, stars, and planets are stitched into. The Big Bang started from a tiny point and expanded outward, creating the fabric of space as it went.

Gahhh!!! If there was nothing there, what did it explode into, then? What was there before it?
Nothing. Before the Bang, space, time, the universe . . . none of it existed. Of course, there may have been other universes . . .

I think I need to lie down.
Good idea. Just relax and think of nothing.

Arghhhhhhhhhhhhhhhhhhhhhh!!!!!!!!!
Sorry.

The Angry Planet

Planet Earth. Third rock from the Sun, 8,000 miles wide, with a mass of around 6,000 trillion tons. It has forests and oceans, mountains and plains, deserts and ice caps. The Earth is a home not only to us, but also to the billions of other animals, plants, fungi, and bacteria we share it with. It's the only known haven for life in the entire solar system—in the universe, even.

So why does it seem so determined to get rid of us?

I mean, seriously, when it's not pelting us with rain and gale-force winds, it's zapping us with lightning and demolishing our houses with earthquakes and tidal waves.

Anyone would think we'd done something to annoy it. Perhaps we have, if global warming is anything to go by.

Let's investigate together ...

Why is the sky blue?

Simple, really. Because the sky is just loads of air stuck to the planet, and air is not see-through; it's blue.

Huh? Wait a minute—I thought air was invisible...

Ah, there's the thing, see. Small amounts of air *are* pretty much clear or transparent (and just very, very slightly bluish). So it *seems* like air is invisible. But if you get a big chunk of air in one place and try to look through it, you see that all that "slightly bluish" adds up to a very real and obvious blue color. And that's what we see in the sky: a massive layer of air, made of billions and billions of very slightly blue air molecules, giving us a beautiful sky-blue ... er ... sky.

Is that it, then? The sky is blue because air is a bit blue?

Pretty much. Same thing goes for the water in lakes and oceans: They look blue because water isn't colorless either; it's very slightly blue. Look down through thousands of tons of it and it looks blue, but scoop out a glass of it and it looks clear. That's why the thin layer of seawater that washes onto the beach with each wave is clear, but the ocean itself is blue.

But I heard the sea is blue because it's reflecting the sky . . .

Sorry—lots of people (including some teachers!) say this, but it simply isn't true. Think about it: Haven't you ever seen a blue sea under a cloudy white or gray sky? Exactly. The sea might not look as bright a blue color on cloudy days, because less light is getting through the clouds to shine into and off the water. But it's still blue, rather than pure gray or white.

But that's simple!

Yes, it is. Of course, if you want to know why air is blue in the first place, then things could get really interesting . . .

Go on, then.

People often use the words *air* and *oxygen* as if they mean the same thing. But while there is plenty of oxygen in air, what we call "air" is actually lots of different gases mixed together. This includes some weird exotic ones like xenon and argon, but it's mostly made of nitrogen (about 78%) and oxygen (about 21%). Anyway—when light from the Sun hits these gas molecules, some of the light goes straight through them, and some of it gets absorbed by the molecules and thrown back out again. Now here's the tricky part: The light from the Sun is white, but white light actually contains all the colors of the rainbow—something scientists call the spectrum of visible light. (Isaac Newton showed us that a few hundred years ago by using glass shapes to split it up).

OK...

Colors all look different to us because they all have different *frequencies.* Don't worry about what *frequency* means for now—it's enough to know that the blue-green end of the light spectrum has a higher frequency than the red-orange end. So yellow light has a higher frequency than red light, green is higher than yellow, blue is higher than green, and so on.

Um... my brain hurts...

Stick with it—we're almost there. Now remember those gas molecules in the air? Well, they tend to absorb and scatter only the high-frequency (or the green and blue) bits of the light that hit them; the low-frequency (red and orange) bits go straight through. So, as light from the Sun comes through the air in the Earth's atmosphere, the blue bits of it get scattered a lot more than the red bits. These blue bits get scattered all over the sky, and so seem to come from everywhere when we look up at it. Hence, the big blue sky.

Got it. But what about sunsets? Then the sky looks red...

At sunset (and sunrise too), the Sun is low on the horizon. When this happens, the light from it has to cut diagonally through the atmosphere (instead of straight down and through, as it does when the Sun is right overhead). This means the light has to come through more air than usual before making it to our eyes. More air means more scattering—and even the red bits get lobbed about this time. So before the Sun's rays are hidden from us at sunset, and just as they start to appear at sunrise, we're treated to a fiery sky full of scattered red light.

Could you dig your way through the Earth to China?

Er . . . no, not really. Even if you could dig that deep, you'd be squashed flat or melted before you got there—by the searing temperatures and crushing pressures inside the planet.

Why's it so hot inside the planet?
Because when the planet was still forming about $4\frac{1}{2}$ billion years ago, its gravity drew in massive amounts of rock and ice in the form of asteroids and comets.* These fiery missiles bombarded the Earth nonstop for thousands of years, and the massive amount of energy released actually melted the planet. It has been cooling down ever since, and while the outside has cooled enough to form a hard crust, the inside is still mostly liquid, or semiliquid (a bit like gooey, melted plastic).

So we live on the crusty part, then?
Exactly. We, and everything else on the Earth, live on that thin shell or crust. This is less than 6 miles thick in some places (like under the deepest ocean trenches), but up to 30 miles thick in others (like under Mount Everest).

* For more about comets and asteroids, see Could comets or asteroids really blow up the Earth if they hit us—like in the movies? (page 43).

If it's so thin, shouldn't it be easy to dig straight through?

Well, the best we've managed so far is a hole about 7 miles deep, drilled over nineteen years from 1970 to 1989, on Russia's Vola Peninsula, near the Norwegian border. At this depth, the temperature was over 572°F, and the drill was damaged as

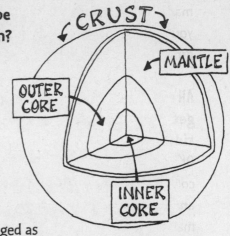

it hit a pocket of molten sulfur. Plus, since the hole wasn't started at the bottom of an ocean trench, this still wasn't enough to make it right through the crust. So, no—it's not that easy.

What if you *could* dig deeper—what would you find?

Beneath the crust is a layer of semimolten rock and metals called the *mantle.* This is about 1,600 miles thick and makes up about two-thirds of the Earth's entire mass. It's mostly made of metals like iron, aluminum, magnesium, and silicon, all held in a gloopy, plastic state at temperatures of over 1832°F.

Beneath that, there's the core of the Earth. This is separated into an *inner core* and an *outer core.* The liquid outer core is about 1,500 miles thick and is mostly made of sulfur and iron. This has a temperature of over 6692°F and flows around the solid inner core. The inner core is made of iron and is even hotter (over 7772°F) than the outer core. But due to a weird effect called pressure freezing, it's actually solid. If you made it down that deep, you'd have a hard time digging through that!

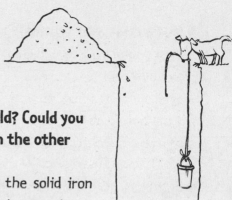

All right, but what if you could? Could you get right through to China on the other side?

OK, let's say you dig through the solid iron core. You survive the burning temperatures and keep going—through the outer core, the mantle, and finally the crust—to the other side. You still wouldn't have made it to China.

Why not?!

Because China isn't exactly opposite the United States on Earth.

What?! Well, what is, then?

Nothing, I'm afraid. Digging straight down from the United States, you'd pop out somewhere in the southern Indian Ocean, between Australia and South Africa. Probably quite annoyed with yourself.

That's not fair.

Sorry. If you check it out on a globe, most tunnels dug from the United States, Europe, or Africa would end up in the ocean. But here are a few transglobal tunnels you could try:

Chile to China
Spain to New Zealand
Brazil to the Philippines
Canada to Antarctica

Bah. Canada to Antarctica? Hardly seems worth the effort.
Unless you're a polar bear. Plenty of tasty penguins down there,
you know . . .

> ## Why don't earthquakes happen everywhere at once?

> Because the ground we live on isn't all in one lump. It's more like a huge rocky jigsaw puzzle floating on a ball of fiery goo. The pieces are moving—but they don't quite fit—and earthquakes happen where they grind against each other.

The ground is floating? On what? The sea?
No, not quite. The "ground" we live on is actually the thin outer
crust of the Earth, which is only a few miles thick in some
places. Being thin, it's also quite brittle and has broken into a
number of jagged-edged plates. But the seas and oceans sit on
top of these. The crusty plates actually sit on the surface of
the mantle.* So this is what the ground floats on.

---

* See *Could you dig your way through the Earth to China?* (page 55) for more about how the
Earth looks on the inside.

Why doesn't it sink?

Because there isn't much of it, and it's not very dense compared to the enormous mass of the mantle beneath it. That said, it does drift around a lot, and it does sink in some places.

How's that happen?

Well, the plates drift around the Earth, grinding and crashing over, under, and against each other all the time. This happens so slowly that we don't notice the movement—but we do see and feel its effects.

Like what?

The changing shape of the world, for one. Billions of years ago, when the planet was first formed, there was one huge sea, and one massive lump of land, which scientists call Pangaea. As the thin crust beneath it cracked, Pangaea broke up, and the pieces drifted apart. Eventually, these pieces became the North American, South American, African, Eurasian (Europe plus Asia), Australasian, and Antarctic continents. You can still see the evidence of this on a world map. If you look at the east coast of South America and the west coast of Africa, you can see that they fit together, more or less, like pieces of a jigsaw puzzle. (The same goes for the east coast of North America and the north coast of Europe, if you twist them around a bit.)

Another effect of all this shifting about was the creation of the world's highest mountain range. The Himalayas were created when the plate carrying India drifted northward and smashed into Asia. The mountain range is literally the result of two plate edges pushing up against each other.

Cool. But what does all that have to do with earthquakes?

Earthquakes are another effect of these crashing, grinding plate edges. Wherever these edges rub against or slip under each other, you get earthquakes. Places like Japan, California, and New Zealand get so many earthquakes because they sit on boundaries (or *fault lines*) between two or more plates.*

But earthquakes are like a back-and-forth shaking thing, aren't they? How do you get that from a sliding plate?

The plates don't slide against each other smoothly. Their jagged, uneven edges get stuck against each other, but the plates keep moving, bending and straining the rocks at the edges. This strain can build up for years, or even hundreds of years, until it finally gives way in one huge, elastic recoil (think of a ruler bent back and let go with a satisfying *poi-oi-ing!!*). An earthquake is the result of this vibration.

So if we know all about these plates and how they move, why can't we predict earthquakes and avoid them?

Sometimes we can predict them. Like the quake set to hit California some time in the next thirty years. We can tell from the strain in the rocks that it'll be a big one, but it's hard to tell exactly when it'll happen, since the equipment and techniques aren't precise enough to allow that just yet. Things have improved, though. In Japan, people used to think earthquakes happened when a giant catfish living underground stirred in his sleep. We've learned a few things since then!

* Japan and New Zealand also have lots of volcanoes for the same reason. See *If lava melts rock, why doesn't it melt the volcano?* (page 61) to find out why.

If lava melts rock, why doesn't it melt the volcano?

Because molten rock only stays hot underground, where it's known as *magma.* Once it gets to the surface, becoming *lava,* it cools down quite quickly. Volcanoes are actually built from this cooling lava in the first place. And while magma won't melt a volcano either, a good buildup can blow its head clean off.

So ... volcanoes are made of lava?

Yes. Well, kind of. Volcanoes are basically holes in the Earth's crust through which gases, ash, and molten rock can escape from the mantle below.* Their huge cones form as magma bubbles out of the vent in the middle, cools, and solidifies. The next blob of magma then bubbles up and outward, over the last bit. Over time, this builds into a cone of solidified rock, with a huge chamber of fresh magma within, and a dome or crater at the top.

Why do they explode?

Many of them don't—they just dribble lava happily down their

* See Could you dig your way through the Earth to China? (page 55) to find out more about the inside of the Earth.

sides for years without erupting. Others may stop flowing for a while as the magma near the top hardens into a rocky cap. Often the magma will then find another way out along the side of the cone, and lava will flow from there instead. But sometimes the magma can't get out, and the pressure beneath the cap builds up over time to enormous levels. When this happens, the cap or dome may be blasted off, forming a huge *pyroclastic cloud* made of hot gas, rock, and ash. This is what makes a volcano truly dangerous. You can stroll away from most lava flows before they reach you, but a pyroclastic cloud can travel at over 100 mph.

That sounds cool! Can I see one?

For an active volcano, your best bet is to head for the islands of the Pacific Ocean.

Why there?

Take a look at the rim of the Pacific Ocean—it's a huge ring taking in the west coast of North and South America from Alaska to Chile; around to New Zealand; up to Hawaii, Borneo, and the Philippines; up through Japan; and back around to Alaska again.

OK...

Well, along this line, you find about three-quarters of the world's volcanoes, and most of the really dangerous active ones. This is because volcanoes form along the boundaries between cracks in the Earth's crust, where magma can ooze through from underneath. These cracks divide the crust into eight major plates (and about twelve smaller ones). The line around the Pacific—known as the "Ring of Fire"—traces the edges of the large Pacific plate, so volcanoes form all around it. In fact Japan, New Zealand, and the Aleutian Islands of Alaska—the ones between the United States and Russia—were built by volcanic activity in the first place. Same goes for the Hawaiian Islands.

So they're, like, fire islands?
Exactly.

Wicked. So where's the best fire?
The Soufrière Hills volcano on the Caribbean island of Montserrat is a good one. It erupted a few years ago and is still belching out enough lava and pyroclastic clouds to make half the island uninhabitable. Another one to watch is Mayon, in the Philippines. This last erupted in 1814 and now looks ready to blow again. The biggest one in recent history was Krakatoa, found on an island close to Java, which erupted in 1883.

What happened then?
It made a bang heard over 3,000 miles away, destroyed over two-thirds of the volcano itself in the explosion, and spewed enough ash into the atmosphere to partially blot out the Sun—dropping temperatures worldwide by 2°F for over three years.

Wow. That's one big kablooie.
You said it.

Where do tsunami come from?

A tsunami is a group of huge waves that forms after an earthquake or a massive landslide. It starts as an immense wall of water that is, quite literally, lifted up out of the ocean. This collapses to form a vast unstoppable train of waves headed straight for the coast . . .

A train of waves? You mean you can get more than one at a time?
Absolutely. In fact, you usually do. For a typical tsunami (or tidal wave, as they're sometimes called), you get between three and five waves striking land at the end of it—not just one.

Why are tsunami so dangerous? I mean, they're only made of water, right?
Quite simply, it's how big they are that makes them dangerous. Because they're so wide (often stretching the entire length of the coastline and beyond), even a $6\frac{1}{2}$-foot tsunami can weigh millions of tons. So rather than imagining "a normal wave—only bigger," try to imagine this: A huge fairytale giant strides through a city, picks up four or five skyscrapers, wades out to sea, and then turns around and starts rolling them up the beach. They crash over houses, trees, and cars, flatten-

ing everything in their path. Now you're somewhere close to seeing the terrifying power of a tsunami.

Whoa. That is pretty scary. But how do they get so big?

Normal waves are formed by the gentle tugging of the Moon's gravity. Even when whipped along a bit by the wind, they don't get very big. Tsunami are different. They're usually formed by undersea earthquakes, around a crack or *fault* in the Earth's crust.* As one side of the crack lifts up during a quake, the whole seabed moves with it, and this lifts a massive wall of water up out of the ocean. This wall has nothing to support it, so it collapses. But as the seabed beneath it is now higher than it was, there's no room for it to fall back into the ocean at the same spot. Instead, it spreads across the surface of the ocean as a series of large waves.

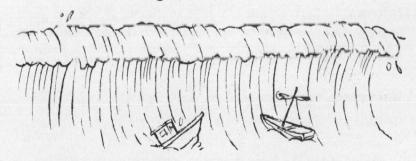

So couldn't you see these coming out at sea and warn people before they hit land?

Well, you can't sit in a boat or helicopter watching the sea all day. And even if you did, you might not spot them.

* For more about earthquakes and faults, see *Why don't earthquakes happen everywhere at once?* (page 58).

Why not?

Out at sea, tsunami waves may be no bigger than 3 feet tall—if you were swimming out there, you could bob right over one and hardly notice it. It's only when they get near the coast that they get bigger. As the waves move up the long, sloping beach or shelf of land near the coast and into shallower water, the first one or two bounce back and reinforce the ones behind, making them bigger. In addition to this, the waves are slowed down by friction as they enter the shallows, dropping speed but increasing in height—up to 100 feet or more. It's these waves (usually the second or third waves in the group) that do the damage as they crash over the land.

How fast are they? Could you outrun one?

Out at sea, the waves can travel at around 440 mph but, as they near the shore, they slow to around 40 mph. So you could outrun one if you had a car or a motorbike. On foot, you'd need a seriously good head start.

What about surfing one?

Forget it. There's no surfing a tsunami, dude.

Boo. Spoilsport. So what does *tsunami* mean, anyway?

It's Japanese. It means "harbor wave."

That doesn't sound very scary.

No, not really. But there's a much better word for the type of tsunami caused by huge landslides or asteroid impacts. These can cause waves up to 1000 feet high, flood entire continents, and wash towns, cities, and whole civilizations off the map forever. They're called mega-tsunami.

That's more like it. That sounds wicked scary.
It does . . . and they are. But thankfully we haven't had one for a few million years.

Phew!

Where does all the water go at low tide?

Into space! Well, kind of. The Earth and its seas are egg-shaped, and water doesn't cover the Earth evenly. High tides happen as we spin through the deep parts. Low tides happen as we spin through the shallows.

What? The Earth is an egg?! I thought it was a ball . . .
Nope. It's almost spherical, but not quite. It's squashed outward around the middle, as if someone is pinching it with a giant thumb and finger at each pole. But in fact, it isn't being squashed at all. It's being stretched out of shape by tidal forces.

Hang on—doesn't *tide* mean "when the sea goes in and out?"

It does. But the tide has to be caused by something, right? Well, that something is a tidal *force*. This is the pulling, stretching, and squashing of one large mass by another one due to gravity. In this case, it's the Earth being pulled out of shape by the Moon and, to a lesser extent, by the Sun.

Er . . . what?

Let's backtrack a bit. We know gravity is a force that pulls objects together, and the bigger the object, the bigger the pull. We also know that the closer together the objects are, the bigger the pull between them.* That OK?

OK . . .

The Moon is a big object, and it's reasonably close to the Earth. So the Moon's gravity constantly tugs at the Earth. But if you think about it, one side of the Earth is a lot closer to the Moon than the other side—about 8,000 miles closer, in fact, since this is how wide the Earth is. So there's a far stronger pull on the moonward side than on the opposite side. This stretches the Earth in the direction of the Moon, making the Earth slightly *oblate* (or egg-shaped), rather than a perfect sphere.

But how does that make the tides happen?

The Moon doesn't just pull on the Earth—it pulls on all the water stuck to the outside of the planet too. The seas and oceans of the Earth form a watery shell around it, but this

---

* If you're not sure how this works, take a look at Why do planets bother going around the Sun? (page 9).

shell isn't spherical either. The water on the moonward side is even closer to the Moon than the Earth it sits on, so it gets pulled toward the Moon more than the water on the opposite side. This makes an egg-shaped watery shell in space, and the Earth itself is pulled into the middle of it. So now you have a squished Earth spinning within a squished ball of water.

Weird.

Slightly, yes. Now here's the fun part: If you imagine (or better yet, draw) these shapes, you'll see that you get an uneven depth of water around the planet. If the water forms an egg shape pointing toward the Moon, then it's deepest at the tip and base of the egg, and shallowest around the sides. Because the Earth spins around once a day, this means one point on it (say, Hawaii) moves alternately through the deeps and shallows twice a day—going deep-shallow-deep-shallow in the course of one turn.

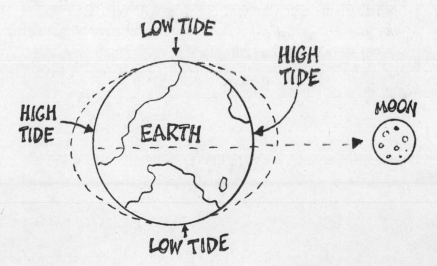

So the island is in deep water twice a day (high tide) and in shallow water twice a day (low tide). And the water at low tide doesn't really "go" anywhere—it just gets shifted around in space.

Cool. But what about the Sun? You said that it pulls on the Earth too?

The Sun does pull on the Earth, and it's much bigger than the Moon. But because it's so much farther away, it doesn't have as much of a tidal (squashing) effect on the planet as the Moon does. It does pull on the oceans a little bit, though, and we see the effects in *spring tides* and *neap tides*. This is when you get extra-high and extra-low tides twice a year, as the Earth moves around the Sun and the pull from the Sun reinforces that of the Moon. If you live by the sea, you may have noticed this.

So if the Moon wasn't there, we'd have no tides?

Pretty much. But the wind would still give us waves, so it wouldn't be all bad. Surf's up, dude!

When lightning strikes the sea, why don't all the fish die?

Mostly because the sea is very deep and wide, so the electricity gets spread out across it before too many of our scaly friends get fried. But some do get zapped occasionally.

So why would some fish get zapped and not others?

Because lightning is basically high-powered electricity belting out of a storm cloud, and electricity behaves in a particular way. It always travels along the easiest path to the ground and—where possible—through materials that let it flow through quickly and easily. Materials that do this are called *conductors*. Seawater is a pretty good conductor, so you might expect that lightning hitting the sea would spread right through it, killing all the fish. But in reality, the lightning spreads out across the surface and probably only fries the fish unlucky enough to be close to the surface (and to the *strike*) when it happens.

Why doesn't it get more of them?

Because there are two things that decide how far an electric current will be carried: One is how well the material conducts it, and the other is how much material it has to go through. The more stuff it has to go through, the more *resistance* there is to the electricity moving through it. There are billions

71

of tons of saltwater in an ocean. So even though saltwater is a good conductor, the electricity would have trouble getting through it all. Instead, it spreads across the surface of the water, heating the water as it goes until the electric charge eventually runs out. This probably happens within about 100 feet of the strike.

So if you're out in a boat, it could still get you 100 feet away?

Definitely. Not a good idea to be out at sea in a thunderstorm, if you can help it. Besides—why would you want to do that? Are you hoping to sit there waiting for a strike, perhaps lobbing in some frozen french fries at the last second to make instant fried fish and chips? A little extreme cooking?

Maybe. Or maybe just to watch it—lightning is cool!

Well, it wouldn't be too smart to try it. Lightning is not to be messed with, believe me.* Even if you are 100 feet away, there's still no guarantee you'll be safe. We know quite a bit about lightning and how it travels through things, but one of the least well-understood phenomena is how it behaves when it hits water. On land, lightning can still be dangerous over 100 feet away from where it strikes. On the water—who knows? For everything we've learned about lightning, there's still a lot we just don't know. It does some truly surprising and confusing things, and *meteorologists* (or weather scientists) still can't quite agree on how or why.

---

* See *Could you survive a lightning strike?* (page 74) to find out why this is.

Like what?

For starters, lightning doesn't always go downward. It can strike upward from ground to cloud. Or sideways—from one cloud to another. Sometimes it forms a ball and floats gently around for a while before disappearing—quite literally—into thin air. When this happens near the ground, it may be mistaken for a ghost or spirit (called "ghost lights" in the United States and Europe, or "min min" by Australian aborigines). But ball lightning can also form high in the sky and may explain some of the UFOs regularly spotted by airline pilots.*

Sweet. So if thunder rolls after lightning, what happens when you roll a lightning ball?

Er—you'd probably lose your fingers in the attempt since the balls are made of super-heated plasma.

What if you wore oven mitts?

Not much use, I'm afraid, since the plasma is at a rather toasty 54,000°F. That's about five times hotter than the surface of the Sun.

Ah. Maybe not, then.

* See *Do UFOs exist, and could my math teacher be an alien?* (page 33) for more about UFOs and ball lightning.

Could you survive a lightning strike?

Plenty of people have—so, yes, it's possible. In fact, some experts think up to 97% of people hit by lightning survive. Even so, I wouldn't want to try it.

Why not? Would you get burned?

That depends on how you get hit. There are several types of lightning strikes, including a *direct strike* (when the lightning bolt hits you full-on), *contact strike* (when it hits something you're touching and the charge flows into you), *splash strike* (when it hits something nearby and the charge jumps into you), and *blunt force strike* (no charge hits you, but you're hit by the shockwave, like a bomb going off a few feet away).

Actually, most lightning victims suffer very few burns, if any at all. When nasty burns do happen, it's usually the result of lightning heating up belt buckles, necklaces, and earrings until they're red hot.

So what do the others look like?

Most lightning injuries look more like the result of an explosion than an electric shock. Like bumps, bruises, broken bones, and ruptured eardrums. For most, clothes and shoes are blasted clean off the victim's body. For some, fingers and toes get blown off too. And there's usually some sort of damage to the eyes.

Ouch. Nasty. So how do you avoid getting hit?

The best way is to stay indoors during thunderstorms, and since most lightning strikes happen before the storm is right on top of you—get inside quickly when they come. Lightning can strike 10 miles or more away from where it's actually raining, so the rule is: If you can hear the thunder, you're in range. So find shelter as soon as you can.

But once you're inside, you're safe?

Mostly, since the structure of the building will generally channel strikes safely to the ground. But it's a good idea to stay off things that are plugged in (like landline phones and computers), since strikes can be conducted into these through the wiring in the walls. And since metal pipes can conduct a lightning strike (quite well, in fact), it's best not to take a shower, wash dishes, or fix the plumbing during a thunderstorm either.

What about if you're outside and there are no houses around? Should you hide in a shed or under a tree or something?

Sheds and trees are no good, I'm afraid. In small structures built without handy metal pipes or wires to conduct the charge safely to the ground, the lightning can rip straight through them and into you. An empty car, however, will do nicely (if it's yours, that is—the police won't take too kindly to your breaking into someone else's car at the first rumble of thunder). A car's metal frame will conduct lightning safely around the passengers to the ground via the tires—though it may knock out the battery and puncture the tires in the process.

But what if there's *nothing* around, and you're, like, out in the middle of a big field or a baseball diamond or something?

Well, you're usually close enough to some kind of shelter to make a break for it in time. If you're really stuck out in the open, it's best to avoid sheltering under trees, telephone poles, or other tall objects. Because lightning seeks the quickest route to the ground (and air isn't itself a great conductor of electricity), it often strikes the tallest object available—so you don't want to be nearby when that happens.

What if *you're* the tallest object around?

Then you should try not to be. If this happens, you're in trouble. As a last resort, you should sit on the ground with your feet together and hope for the best.

Hope for the best? Isn't there anything else you could do?

Well, you could try and make friends with as many tall people as possible and hang out with them all the time, just in case.

What?! Now you're just being stupid.

Hey, I'm not the one stuck out in a field in the middle of a thunderstorm . . .

Where does wind come from, and where is it going?

Wind comes from the churning movement of air heated up by the Sun. It moves from the equator to the poles and back again. It breezes in from the sea by day, and breezes back out again at night. Wind is always going somewhere, but it never quite arrives . . .

What do you mean, "it never quite arrives"?

Think about it—there isn't one super windy place on the planet that collects wind. (Although if there were, Chicago would surely be a strong contender.) Some places are windier than others, and you could say that wind begins life at the equator. But wind doesn't travel somewhere and just stop dead. It moves in a constant cycle around the planet, moving from areas of high to low air pressure in an effort to balance out the air pressures around the globe.

Why does wind start off at the equator?

Well, wind is simply a movement of air from one place to another, at a variety of speeds ranging from gentle breeze through gale- and hurricane-force winds. It doesn't really start anywhere, but the forces that drive the movement begin at the equator.

But why there?

Because this is where the air pressure first starts to shift around, kicking off the whole wind cycle. You may have noticed that countries near the equator are warmer than those nearer the poles. This is because the areas around the equator receive more direct and more constant sunlight than those farther from it.* This heats up the air at the equator and, because hot air rises, it drifts up like an invisible balloon into the atmosphere, leaving a gap—or area of lower air pressure—beneath it. So more air nearer the ground rushes in to fill the gap. This rushing air, quite simply, is wind.

Now the warm air higher up has to go somewhere. Depending on which side of the equator it is, it either drifts north or south, toward the poles. But it doesn't get there in one trip. After traveling about 30° north or south of the equator—about one-third of the way to the poles—it cools off and starts to sink down to the ground again. Some of this cooler air then makes its way back to the equator, filling the "gap" left by the air still warming and rising there. This makes a little mini-circuit or *wind cell* between the equator and the tropics, 30° north and south of it. More cells form between 30° and 60°, another one beyond that, and so on, until you get a chain of cells all the way to the poles and back. The wind follows the shifting air, blowing north to south and south to north within these cells.

* See *If countries are hotter in the south, why doesn't the South Pole melt?* (page 92) for more on why this is so.

But wind normally comes from the east or west, doesn't it? That's what the weatherman is always saying . . .
You're right—the more common (or prevailing) winds often come from the east or west, depending on where you live.

That's because we've forgotten something. The Earth doesn't stay still during all this heating by the Sun—it's spinning around too, so the air has to go with it. This creates a force (called the Coriolis force) that puts a spin on the rising and falling air, making the wind cycle within each cell travel clockwise or counterclockwise, instead of straight up and down. So you end up with a complex pattern of moving air, with alternating bands around the Earth having either westerly or easterly prevailing winds.

And what about sea breezes? Wherever you are in the world, the wind blows in from the sea, doesn't it?
That's true, it does. But not very strongly, hence "sea breeze" rather than "sea blast" or "sea gale," which suggests that this is caused by a smaller set of forces. It actually happens because the land heats up and cools down faster than the sea does. So as the air over land heats up during the day, it rises, leaving a pressure gap for the cooler air over the sea to flow into—creating a sea breeze. At night, the reverse happens: The land cools faster, and the warmer air over the sea is replaced by air from the land. This creates a breeze that goes out to sea at night, and the whole thing works like a kind of mini-wind-cycle along the shore.

I can make wind all by myself, you know . . .
That's something else entirely. And just make sure you're downwind of me when you do it.

When do storms turn into hurricanes?

When storm clouds form over warmer waters, when the wind is just right, and when the planet gives the clouds some extra spin . . . *then* you get a hurricane. Thankfully, not too often in most parts of the United States.

But some places get them every year, don't they?
That's true. While most places get storms, only a few seem to get regular hurricanes. For example, hurricanes hit countries around the Gulf of Mexico—like Cuba, the Caribbean islands, and the southeastern United States—every year around the same time. This is called a hurricane "season." Likewise, Japan has a season when it is pounded by typhoons, and India has a season of cyclones.

What's the difference between a hurricane, a typhoon, and a cyclone, anyway?
There is no difference—technically, they are all types of *tropical cyclones*. The only difference is where in the world you find

them. If a tropical cyclone forms in the Atlantic Ocean, we call it a hurricane. If it forms in the Pacific, it's a typhoon. And if it forms in the Indian Ocean, we just call it (perhaps most sensibly) a cyclone. But they're all the same thing.

So why in those places, and why so often?

A hurricane (typhoon, cyclone, whatever) can only form over warm, tropical waters, in a moist atmosphere, fanned by certain types of wind. This only occurs in seven regions on the planet—one in the Atlantic, three in the Pacific, and three more in the Indian Ocean. These are the *tropical cyclone* basins where these monster storms are born.

Why does warm water make a difference?

Because it's warm water evaporating into water vapor that feeds a hurricane. As the water vapor rises into the atmosphere, it cools and condenses into droplets of rain. In doing so, they give their heat into the air around them, making it lighter and causing it to rise. As the warm air rises, it leaves a pressure "gap" underneath it, which fresh air rushes in to fill. This rushing air is the powerful wind that we associate with hurricanes. This also explains why hurricanes lose power as they move over land from the sea—because they can no longer "feed" off the warm waters evaporating beneath them.

Why do they look like big, spinning doughnuts when you see them on satellite pictures?

Because the clouds don't stay still—they're given a spin by the Coriolis force.* This creates a huge mass of swirling cloud ro-

* For more about how this works, see Where does wind come from, and where is it going? (page 77).

81

tating around a central "eye." Depending on which side of the equator they form on, they either spin clockwise or counterclockwise.

Is it true that it's calm in the eye of a hurricane?

Yes, it is. Because the hurricane is turning, it generates a force (called a centrifugal force) that flings clouds and water vapor outwards, preventing winds from approaching the very center. So the winds get as close as they can, raging around the center but not in it. This creates a calm, quiet eye (usually between 10 and 50 miles wide) in the middle, but with an ultraviolent, super-windy *eye wall* around it. If a hurricane moves right over you, the winds become incredibly violent, then calm, then violent again. So you still don't really want to be in there.

What was the worst one ever?

The strongest on record was Hurricane Wilma, in 2005, which had winds of up to 175 mph. But in terms of damage done, Wilma was pretty kind compared to Hurricane Andrew, which did about $26 billion worth of damage when it hit Florida in 1992. Then, of course, Hurricane Katrina devastated New Orleans in 2005, causing $45 million worth of damage and leaving thousands of people homeless.

Pretty scary, huh?

Yup. And it almost certainly won't be the last time that happens, either. In spite of all our power and technology, hurricanes remind us just how small and fragile we humans really are . . .

What would it be like inside a tornado?

That depends on how you got in there, and how big the tornado was. Ordinarily, getting sucked into a tornado would be a terrifying experience. But if you somehow managed to get inside safely, it would be noisy, yet eerily still.

Noisy but still? That's a bit weird, isn't it?

Well, tornadoes are weird. Unlike volcanoes, tsunami, and hurricanes, we still don't know that much about them, despite years of research.

So what are they, and what *do* we know about them?

Tornadoes are violently rotating columns of air that extend down to the ground from certain types of cloud, called *cumuliform* clouds. Sometimes—but not always—you can see them, and they look like huge spinning funnels in the sky. Sometimes they're all but invisible, and all you can see is the debris they fling around. They often form from rotating storm systems called *supercells,* which can occur either on their own or on the edges of hurricanes, typhoons, and cyclones.*

---

* See *When do storms turn into hurricanes?* (page 80) for more about how these can form.

Why do they only happen in the United States?

While tornadoes seem to be most common in the United States, they do occur elsewhere. They seem to be fairly common in China and India (where typhoons and cyclones are also quite common); in fact, they can occur more or less anywhere.

Really? But I've never seen one . . .

Well, the United States gets around a thousand tornadoes every year, and in fact, every mainland state gets at least a few of them each year. But tornadoes appear mostly in the states between the Rocky and Appalachian mountains, an area nicknamed "tornado alley" (Texas, Oklahoma, and Alabama get the most). So unless you live in this area, you can go for years or decades without happening upon a tornado. And you may never see a really powerful one.

So how big and powerful do they get?

The power of a tornado is measured on a scale called the Fujita scale, which goes from F0 to F5. The scale measures the damage done by a tornado, rather than its size or wind speed. So an F0 (light damage) topples chimneys but leaves the roof on your house, an F3 (severe damage) will uproot forests and fling cars about, and an F5 (incredible damage) will lift an entire house off the ground. In the United States, F5 tornadoes strike almost every year.

Scary. But what would it feel like to be picked up by one?

Not good. First of all, you'd hear it coming. Tornadoes usually sound something like the low rumble of a passing train, but if the funnel is noisily ripping up wood, steel, and concrete as it goes, these sounds can combine into a deafening roar.

The awesome power of a tornado, with wind speeds topping 300 mph, can turn small harmless objects like pencils and pebbles into deadly bullets. These are flung outward from the funnel as it approaches, strafing nearby objects like machine-gun fire. Most tornado injuries come from this flying debris rather than the tornado itself. But if you managed to avoid the debris and enter the funnel, you would be caught in the updraft and flung 300 feet into the air, along with anything else it picked up. Heavy objects like cars usually land 10 to 20 feet away. Clothing and pieces of paper picked up by tornadoes have been known to land over 60 miles away. You'd probably land somewhere in between.

So why is it calm right in the middle of one? Is it like the eye of a storm or a hurricane?
It's similar in that the wind is prevented from entering by the spinning motion of the funnel, which creates an "eye" in the center. It would be calm because, theoretically (no one has seen this and lived), the wind on one side of the eye would be going at 100 mph or more in one direction, and on the other side at an equal speed but in the opposite direction. This means that the wind speed somewhere near the middle would be zero. So, for a second or two, you'd hear the roaring power of the tornado, but you wouldn't feel it. But unlike hurricanes—which have eyes more than 10 miles wide—most tornado "eyes" are only 3 feet or so across. So you'd probably be in and out before you had time to notice how nice and calm it was.

So that's what it'd be like inside a tornado.
Terrifying.

Gotcha. Think I'll pass.

Know your stuff: storms, cyclones, and hurricanes

Storm: A disturbance in the Earth's atmosphere that affects its surface—usually through strong winds, heavy rain, and possibly thunder, lightning, ice, snow, or hail. Storms can be light, moderate, severe, or extreme, depending on the wind speed.

Cyclone: Organized, rotating storm system that forms over tropical or subtropical waters. There are various types of cyclones, which are given different names depending on which ocean they form over. To be a true cyclone, the wind speed must be over 75 mph—anything slower than that is a tropical depression.

Tropical cyclone or cyclonic storm: A cyclone that forms over the Indian or southwest Pacific Ocean.

Typhoon: A cyclone that forms over the northwest Pacific Ocean.

Hurricane: A cyclone that forms over the Atlantic or northeast Pacific Ocean.

Tornado: A violently rotating column of air.

> ## Is the Earth really getting hotter, and is that so bad?

> The world is definitely getting hotter—it'll probably get between 2° and 11°F hotter over the next 100 years. That might not seem so bad, but if you think of all the stuff that comes with it, you see why too much "global warming" is a very bad thing.

Hold on—I thought scientists were still arguing whether it's happening or not . . .

No, not at all. Almost everyone agrees that "global warming" is happening. It's just how fast it's happening, whether it will continue, how far it will go, and whether or not we're causing it that we're still not sure about.

I don't get it.

Global warming—the planet getting progressively hotter over time—is caused by a process called the "greenhouse effect." In simple terms, this happens because the Earth's atmosphere is transparent to sunlight, but not to the heat that comes off the Earth as sunlight heats it up. So the heat is held inside the atmosphere, raising the temperature. This is a bit like the way the glass of a greenhouse lets light in and out but stops heat from escaping, allowing us to grow warm-weather plants in colder countries. Hence the name "greenhouse effect." This idea isn't even particularly new. The Irish physicist and mountaineer John Tyndall first described it in 1863—along with a few other things, like why the sky is blue.* He and other scientists also realized that this effect is so important in maintaining global temperatures that there probably wouldn't be life on the planet without it.

Why's that?
Well, thanks to the greenhouse effect, the Earth's atmosphere is far hotter than it would be through direct heating from sunlight alone. Without it, the Earth's surface would be about 59°F colder than it is—around 0°F. This simply wouldn't be warm enough to support all the bacterial, plant, and animal life that lives on it.

So it's all good, then? What's the problem?
The problem is that lately this warming effect seems to have been intensifying and speeding up. We think at least part of this might be due to gases spewed out by our cars, planes, factories, and power plants, among other things. So most of the arguments about global warming are about whether we should replace or cut down on using these things in order to slow down the pace of the effect. In any case, at the current rate, it looks as if global temperatures will rise by about 2° to 11°F by the year 2100.

* See Why is the sky blue? (page 52) if you want to know why!

By 2 degrees? That doesn't sound so bad.

Maybe not, but even this small rise will have a serious effect on countries all over the world.

Like what?

At the very least, there will be a small rise in sea levels world-wide due to faster-melting ice at the poles and the oceans expanding as they heat up. This will cause flooding of farm-lands on low-lying coastlines and islands. More heating of the oceans will probably lead to a general increase in severe weather like hurricanes, typhoons, and tornadoes. Countries around the equator will get warmer and drier, causing more droughts. Countries farther from the equator will get warmer and wetter, attracting mosquitoes (they love warm, wet en-vironments) and all the deadly diseases they carry. Some argue that we're already seeing these effects today. And that isn't the worst of it.

That doesn't sound good. Go on, then—what's the worst that could happen?

Well, everything we've said so far is our best guess of what will happen, based on what we know about how the Earth's atmosphere and oceans interact. But things could get more complicated, and (as we often see with simple weather fore-casts) predictions about how the atmosphere and oceans will behave can be wrong. It's possible (although unlikely) that the increased heating of the seas could release enough water va-por into the atmosphere to create a "runaway greenhouse ef-fect," pushing temperatures up so high that trees and crops across the world would die. On the other hand, if enough polar ice melted and diluted the oceans, it could affect the way they circulate (through currents) across the world. One result of this might be stopping or reversing the flow of the Gulf Stream—the current that supplies Europe with warm water—plunging Europe and the United Kingdom into long, freezing winters similar to those in the Arctic. We know this has happened in the past (about 8,000 years ago), so it could well happen again.

But if we don't know for sure what will happen, what can we do to stop it?

Good point. We don't know for sure. And maybe nothing *can* stop it. But we know the world's getting hotter, and we're fairly sure human activity is playing at least some part in that. So, if there's a chance we can make a difference, then most countries argue that it's better to be careful until we find out more.

Like "better safe than sorry"?

Exactly. Or alternatively: "If we ain't wise, then maybe we fries."

If countries are hotter in the south, why doesn't the South Pole melt?

Because the South Pole is as cold as the North. Not all countries are hotter in the south—only those on the top half of the Earth, like the United States and Russia. Those on the bottom, like Chile and New Zealand, get colder the farther south you go. It's how far you are from the middle that counts.

Hang on a minute—that can't be right. I know for a fact Australia is very hot, and that's pretty far south, isn't it?
It's not that far south, actually. Its northern edge is only about 10° south of the equator, and the southern edge is only about 40° south—that's less than halfway between the equator and the South Pole. Even so, it's colder in the south of Australia than it is in the north.

But that's the opposite of here, isn't it? Here, you get snow mostly in the north, and it's much warmer in the south...
That's right. But that's because we're in the northern half (or hemisphere) of the Earth, while Australia is in the southern half.

Why should that make a difference?

Because it's not really about how far north and south you are—it's how far away from the equator a place is that tells you how hot or cold it's likely to be.

Yeah, I kind of knew that already. But why? I mean, what is the equator, anyway? I thought it was just the line around the middle of the Earth. Or the middle of the map.

It is. But it also marks out a band around the Earth that gets the most direct sunlight all year long.

How's that?

Imagine you could draw a big circle in space, sketching out the path of the Earth as it orbits the Sun. Now color in the circle—let's go with yellow—making a huge, yellow disk. Half the Sun is poking out above the disk and half below it. Same goes for the Earth—the disk looks like it's chopping the planet in half. Got it?

Got it.

Now let's say the equator is on that line which divides the Earth in two. Imagine sticking a skewer right through the Earth from top to bottom and turning it around and around, like you're grilling a kebab. When the disk turns, the Earth orbits around the Sun but also spins on its axis (or kebab skewer). Hopefully you can now see why: If the Earth was a giant meatball or kebab, then the ring around the middle (the equator) would get heated up more than the bits nearer the stick (the poles)—simply because they're closer to the heat source (or Sun's rays), represented by the big yellow disk.

Gotcha. So places near the equator get more of a grilling than those farther away?

Exactly. And it doesn't matter which direction away from the equator you go—farther north and farther south both take you closer to the skewer, and farther away from the grill. That's why South Africa is colder than Zimbabwe, why New Zealand is colder than Australia and why New Zealand's South Island is colder than the North Island.

Is that it, then?

Not quite. In our orbiting meatball/kebab model, the skewer (or axis of the Earth) is pointing straight up and down. The Earth is actually tilted at an angle of about 23° away from the vertical. So, instead of the equator being level with the big yellow disk, it's tilted at 23° to it.

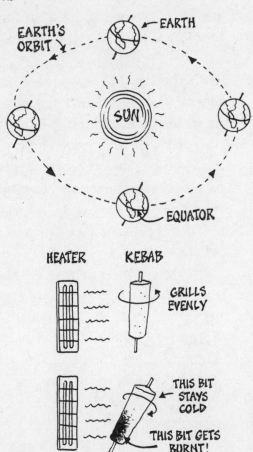

EARTH'S ORBIT

EARTH

SUN

EQUATOR

HEATER   KEBAB

GRILLS EVENLY

THIS BIT STAYS COLD

THIS BIT GETS BURNT!

So what does that mean?

That means the grilling rays of the Sun are not focused on the equator all year round. They spend half the year directly toasting the part just above the equator, and the other half of the year toasting the part beneath it. The rays are only focused right on the equator itself twice a year—as they pass from one side of it to the other. This is what gives us the four seasons. When our half of the Earth (the Northern Hemisphere) is tilted away from the Sun, the southern half gets more of a grilling and it's summer down there. But we get less of a grilling, so it's winter for us. When we're tilted toward the Sun, the reverse happens—summer for us, but winter for those in the Southern Hemisphere. Spring and autumn are the bits in between. All because the Earth spins on a tilted axis (or skewer).

So what would happen if the axis wasn't tilted?

Then we'd have no changing of the seasons. It would be like permanent summer near the equator, and permanent winter for Canada, Peru, New Zealand, and most countries in Europe.

Nice if you like skiing and snowball fights. Not so nice, however, if you don't like igloos, polar bears, and hypothermia.

Did people ski during the Ice Age?

Technically, we're still in an ice age, so yes! Aside from that, skiing is at least 5,000 years old. The last real ice age ended about 10,000 years ago, and people may have skied in China even then.

What do you mean, "we're still in an ice age"? No, we're not!
Yes, we are.

Are not!
Are too! Look, this is stupid. As a matter of fact, we're both right—it depends what you mean by *ice age*.

Huh?
Let me explain. The Earth hasn't always been the same temperature, right? But there was more than one "ice age," or period of time when ice covered large areas of the planet. In fact, for the last 4 billion years, the Earth has been heating up and then cooling down again in a fairly regular way, with most of it freezing over and melting again every 100,000 years or so. This happens as changes in the Earth's atmosphere cause the global temperatures to go up and down in waves or cycles.

Why does that happen?

Well, we think it's partly due to changes in how much radiation the Sun puts out and to small changes in the Earth's orbit around it. We think of these things as pretty constant, but they can change over long periods of time. When the Earth's changing orbit takes it even slightly farther away from the Sun, it causes a big drop in temperature—so this could be enough to trigger an ice age in itself. This cooling and warming effect could also be affected by certain gases in the atmosphere (like methane, water vapor, and carbon dioxide). These contribute in different ways to the heating of the Earth caused by the "greenhouse effect."* As the levels of these gases change—due to volcanic eruptions, meteorite impacts, or just natural shifts in their cycles through the environment—the whole Earth's surface temperature changes along with them. So these could be a factor too.

In any case, when the temperature drops, the ice—held in huge glaciers at the North and South Poles—extends toward the equator. In fact, some scientists think that around 600 million years ago the glaciers may have extended all the way to the equator—turning the Earth into a giant snowball!

Cool! But wouldn't that have killed everything on the planet?

Not necessarily—although this may have caused the extinction of hundreds of thousands of plants and animals. We can't be sure that it happened this way, but if it did, much of the

* See *Is the Earth really getting hotter, and is that so bad?* (page 88) for details of how this works.

sea life (at least) would have survived under the ice, waiting for the big thaw. A big thaw always follows a big freeze in the cycle.

So what happens then?

When the temperature rises again, the glaciers melt and the edge of the ice draws back to the poles again, leaving two huge ice "caps" rather than melting away completely. The term *ice age* is used to describe any period of time when ice sheets are present in the Northern and Southern Hemispheres. By that definition, we're still in one, as ice sheets have covered Greenland and Antarctica for the last 40 million years.

More commonly, though, we use the term to describe periods in time when ice covers most of Europe and North America. The last time this happened was about 10,000 years ago. So we often refer to that as "the last ice age."

Fine. You win. So did people ski back then, or what?

We don't know for sure, but possibly, yes. Carvings and pictures drawn on cave rocks show that people were definitely using skis to get around in Norway and other countries around the Arctic Circle over 4,000 years ago. Recently, similar pictures have been found in northwestern China, and the Chinese claim that these are over 10,000 years old—right when the last ice age ended. So yes—it's possible that people skied out of the last ice age.

So the Chinese invented it?

That we don't know. What we do know is that the oldest skis in existence—between 4,000 and 5,000 years old—were found in Sweden and Finland. We also know that the Vikings of northern Europe worshipped a god and goddess of skiing, and that the Romans found people skiing when they invaded Finland about 2,000 years ago. The Romans then introduced it as they conquered the rest of Europe. After that, it didn't make it to North America, it seems, until about one hundred years ago, when Norwegian miners moved there for work, taking their sport with them.

What about ski jumping? Did cavemen do it by skiing off the backs of dinosaurs?

Sadly, no. The dinosaurs were pretty much wiped out about 65 million years before humans came around. So we've never really shared the same planet with them.* Woolly mammoths, though, lived until about 4,000 years ago, so a particularly brave caveman might have jumped off one of them.

Ha! That sounds like fun.

Not if you're a mammoth.

---

* At least, the big ones you could ski off were wiped out. See *Why are there no dinosaurs any more?* (page 131) for details.

Animal
Answers

Animals are amazing, aren't they?

Even though we think of ourselves as the smartest and best creatures on the planet, there are still plenty of things other animals can do that we can't.

Among them, there are those that can move faster, dive deeper, see and hear farther than we could ever hope to. Some can even change color, and others can paralyze us with deadly poisons.

But we're leaving that stuff for the wildlife document-aries. Here we explore the real mysteries of the animal kingdom, such as: Do they talk? Do they get sunburned? Do they fart?

And why do some of them seem so lame? If dolphins are so clever, why haven't they learned to breathe underwater? If dinosaurs were so terrifying, why aren't there any left? And—I ask you—what is the point of a flightless bird?

All this and more will be revealed.

Do rabbits fart?

Quite simply—yes. In fact, nearly all animals do, since it's a necessary part of digesting food.

Nearly all animals?

Well, almost. If by "fart" you mean "release gas from the gut," then all animals with guts will, in fact, fart. Insects, fish, lizards, snakes, cats, dogs, mice, elephants . . . almost any creature you can think of. In fact, the only ones that don't fart are those that didn't evolve guts—like sponges, jellyfish, and some types of worm. Guts are for taking in food and plopping out waste products, and these animals either absorb food through the surface of their bodies, or eat and poop through the same hole.

Gross. I think I'd rather have guts.

Absolutely. But then you have no choice but to fart. As food is digested in the gut, gases are made from the chemical reactions inside. So it's either fart or starve for most animals. Including us.

Really?! You mean you *have* to fart? That's fantastic!

Again, that depends on what you mean by "fart." If you mean "release gas from your bottom," then, yes—you have to. It's happening all the time, whether you like it or not. But if you mean "trumpet loudly and award yourself a score out of ten," then no—this isn't strictly necessary.

Phooey! So farts are just food gas from our guts, then?

Well, that's not the whole story. Most animals (including us) also have bacteria living in their guts that release more gases as they too break down food. Many animals—particularly plant eaters like rabbits—couldn't live without these bacteria in their guts. For land animals, some fart gas also comes from air swallowed accidentally with food. All this gas has to go somewhere, so it gets pushed along with the food to the animal's bottom . . . and you know the rest. Of course, some animals fart more than others.

OK—which ones? I have to know . . .

Some animals produce so much fart gas that it spreads around the Earth's atmosphere and plays a role in global warming.* Scientists used to think cows were one of the worst, but it turns out that it's probably their burps, rather than their farts, that do it. Termite farts, on the other hand, produce more methane (one of the gases involved in global warming) than all of our cars, planes, and factories put together! The termites can't help this, of course. It's because they need

* See *Is the Earth really getting hotter, and is that so bad?* (page 88) for more details of how this works.

more of those gut bacteria than most animals in order to digest their woody diet. But it has earned them the number one spot in our *Top 10 animals that fart* list. The rest are in no particular order, other than how stinky I've found them to be.

Top 10 animals that fart

1	Termites
2	Camels
3	Zebras
4	Sheep
5	Cows
6	Elephants
7	Labradors/Retrievers
8	Humans (vegetarian)
9	Humans (others)
10	Gerbils

Can animals talk, and what do they say?

Plenty of them can—although not exactly the way we do. We still can't understand most of them, or what they're saying, but a lot of it seems to be about food, fighting, and *loooooove*.

Can't some of them talk like we do, like parrots? I even saw a cat say "hello" once on the Internet.

Animals don't have the same equipment as we do for talking. Many have tongues, of course—but tongues are just for shaping the sounds of words that start as vibrations in our throats. Most animals lack complex vocal cords like we have in our throats, so they can't make smooth vowel sounds. Parrots and a few other animals can make noises that sound like words, but they're really just mimicking us, and they don't really understand what they're saying.

How do they talk, then?

Lots of animals can "talk" by making noises that they can understand, even if we can't. Birds do this when they chirp and sing, cats when they meow and purr, and dolphins when they click and whistle. Many of these noises translate to simple phrases like "I'm hungry," "I'm angry," "feed me," and "leave me alone." But some may be quite complex: Dolphins chatter to each other constantly as they play, and seem to give each other instructions when they hunt fish together in groups.

Other animals use signals and sign language to talk to each other. Bees do a complicated dance to tell other bees in which direction to go to find food. To us, it just looks like a figure eight with a bum-waggle in the middle. But if the bee "draws" the eight upright, it means "head toward the Sun"; if it draws it at an angle, that tells the other bees at what angle from the Sun they should head away from the hive. (So, for example, an eight on its side would mean "head off at 90° to the Sun.") A gorilla leading a troop through the forest will do a similar thing—by thumping two trees, one after the other. The line between the two trees tells the other gorillas which way they're headed for the day, and they all understand at once.

Not bad. But that's not real sign language, is it? It's still just giving directions. What about words and sentences?

Scientists have managed to teach a few chimpanzees some basic, human-style sign language. But they can only do a few words and don't seem good at putting sentences together. It may be that only humans have evolved the bits of brain that deal with making and understanding whole sentences. Or it could be that animal sentences just look different.

How d'you mean?

Well, dolphins and whales have pretty complex brains too, and we still don't understand what all their clicks and whistles mean, so they could be talking in full sentences for all we know. Some types of octopus and squid might even be able to do it. Some cuttlefish can hold "conversations" with up to four friends at once, by using different sides of their bodies to make patterns of light and color*—patterns that change so fast we can hardly see them. Could be a lot going on there.

Will we ever be able to understand them?

Maybe, one day. It's possible that in the future we'll have computers so powerful that they'll be able to decode the dolphin clicks—even translate Cuttlefish into English.

Crazy. I wonder what they'll say?

Maybe something like: "Do you mind? I wasn't talking to you ..."

NICE DAY

PURR-FECT!

* See *How many colors can a chameleon do?* (page 108) to find out how they do this.

How many colors can a chameleon do?

Hundreds, if you count different shades of the same color. But most of the time, they just stick to a few: green, brown, gray, and cream (with yellow spots).

But I thought they could do tons of colors . . .

True, some of them can. But just because they can, doesn't mean they do. Unless they've got a good reason, most chameleons are happy enough as they are. Some couldn't change much even if they wanted to—the best pygmy chameleons from West Africa can do is a few measly shades of brown.

That's stupid. If I were a chameleon, I'd be doing it all the time. Blue, orange, pink, purple . . .

Would you? Let's think about it: Why do chameleons change color?

To blend in with their surroundings?

Well, that's one reason. And which colors would you need to blend into the jungles of Madagascar—where most chameleons live?

You'd need green. And brown. And, er . . . well, that's it, really.

And that's why they don't bother much with bright red or yellow.

But occasionally, they *will* turn crazy, bright colors.

Why? To look like fruit?

Not quite. Camouflage isn't the only reason chameleons change color, you know. In fact, it's not the main reason at all.

So why else would they do it?

They also do it as they respond to changes in light and temper-ature. And sometimes their color changes with their mood.

So what does each color mean, then?

Green or brown are usually a chameleon's natural color. It uses these colors to blend in with the colors of tree leaves, bark, and branches.

If it's cream or yellow, it's either trying to cool off (as lighter colors reflect more sunlight) or it's angry (perhaps lit-erally telling others "watch out—I need to cool off!").

Any other colors will usually mean it's either threatening someone or flirting with someone. So you could think of these colors usually bright ones, like red or blue—as war paint or fancy makeup.

Can any other animals change color?

Quite a few, in fact. Even if you don't count animals that change their coat color with the seasons (of which there are many), there are several types of spiders, fish, and octopuses that can change color quickly when hunting or hiding.

Which one's the best at it?

Probably cuttlefish. They are truly amazing to watch.

A chameleon can change color completely in about ten or fifteen seconds, by moving layers of colored pigment in its skin cells. It uses a few basic colors of pigment to produce lots of colors.

A cuttlefish has millions of these pigment cells—like the colored dots that make up the picture on a computer screen—and it can blink each one "on" and "off" as quickly and easily as we can blink an eyelid. So it can change color hundreds of times per second—making colors move in waves, and creating flowing "pictures" and images on its skin. It's as if its thoughts are rippling over its skin, like a living television.

Freaky. I wonder if they can pick up *"Big Brother"*?

What do people taste like to sharks and tigers?

Probably quite tasty. A bit like beef, only sweeter. Thankfully, though, sharks and tigers almost never eat people—they like seals and deer much better.

Sweet beef? Ugh!

Well, you asked. And what did you expect? Chicken?

All mammals have pretty much the same proteins to build their muscles. It's just the number and type of muscle fibers that give meat from different animals a slightly different taste and texture. So horse is a bit chewier than cow, whale a bit saltier than cow, and we're ... well, a bit sweeter.

So that's how we taste to sharks and tigers: sweet and beefy?

Something like that. But we can't really say for sure, since they might interpret the taste differently. In any case, we can't be that tasty because they don't seem to want to eat us much.

But they eat people all the time, don't they?

Not at all. Tiger and shark attacks on people are actually very rare and, even when they do attack, tigers and sharks almost

MMM... TASTES LIKE CHICKEN...

never eat their victims. Believe it or not, tigers usually run away from people and only attack if they're attacked first, cornered, or surprised. Even then they usually just claw at or bite their victims and walk off— they don't stick around to chew and swallow.

As for sharks, only a few types—like great whites, bull sharks, and tiger sharks—attack people. The rest generally ignore people. Even these "killer" sharks will avoid people wherever they can, and most shark attacks are not on divers or swimmers (as you might expect), but on surfers.

Why? What do they have against surfing?

Nothing that we know of—it's just that when surfers paddle out into the waves on their boards, they look a lot like seals from underneath. Sharks like seals. Seals are delicious. So imagine how disappointed they are when they take a bite out of a surfboard (or, occasionally, a surfer) and find out that seal's off the menu. They're usually disgusted and swim off in a huff.

These "bump and run" attacks make up over 90% of reported shark assaults on people. And the victims usually survive.

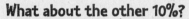

What about the other 10%?

Er . . . well, they're unlucky enough to be scarfed by sharks in a feeding frenzy. That can happen when a group of sharks smells blood in the water. But again—it's very rare. Sharks don't kill anywhere near as many people per year as jellyfish do. And, on land, tigers kill far fewer people than hippos do.

No way! Are they the most dangerous animals, then?

Not by a long shot. On land, mosquitoes kill way more people than any other animal, and in the sea jellyfish are second to a kind of big snail called a cone shell. Check out our *Top 10 killer animals* list.

Top 10 killer animals

The mosquito carries microorganisms in its spit that cause malaria and a whole range of other nasty diseases, including dengue fever. These diseases kill over 3 million people across the globe every year.

The cone shell is a pretty, snaillike mollusk that fires a venomous harpoon from the end of its shell at anyone silly enough to pick it up. Stings can kill in seconds.

The sea wasp, also known as the box jellyfish, trails its 16-foot-long tentacles in the water. Its stingers can kill in hours.

The spitting cobra is a very venomous, very aggressive snake found in India. It kills over 50,000 people a year.

The taipan is a venomous snake—with poison eighty times more powerful than a rattlesnake's—from Australia. Thankfully, only four or five people a year get bitten.

The funnel web spider is far more dangerous than the famous black widow. Its venom can kill a person in less than fifteen minutes. Cats and dogs are immune, though, so if you see one, set Fido or Tiddles on it.

The hippo, incredibly, kills more people in Africa than any other wild animal—most of them in small boats. (The people, not the hippos.)

The killer bee is an aggressive mutant crossbreed of African and South American bees. Swarms may chase victims for miles—often provoked by lawnmowers.

The elephant kills more than 500 people a year in Africa—way more than lions or leopards.

The poison dart frog is tiny, but each little frog contains enough poison in its skin to kill ten to twenty people.

Can animals see and hear things we can't?

Absolutely—lots of them can. Some can see in infrared and ultraviolet. Others can "see" objects just by listening for them. On the flipside, most mammals are color-blind, and most insects are completely deaf.

So some animals have better senses than us, and others have worse?

It's difficult to compare them like that, as each one has evolved senses to best suit its needs and environment. Moles, for example, have incredible senses of hearing and touch, but are practically blind. So, on balance, they're probably no better or worse off than us—just different. But, individually, some animals do have some pretty incredible abilities.

Like what? Like, which animal can see the best?

That depends what you mean by "see." If you mean "best eyesight," then birds of prey are pretty incredible. Andean condors can spot rabbits from 3 miles away, and falcons still see them clearly even when diving at over 125 mph.

If you mean "see things we can't," then bees can see

ultraviolet light (as a shade of violet—scientists call it "bee purple"), and some snakes can "see" the infrared heat trails of their victims—a bit like those night-vision goggles used by soldiers.

Sweet. What about super-hearing? Dogs are pretty good, aren't they?

Dogs can certainly hear higher-pitched sounds than us. We can hear sounds of up to around 20,000 hertz (hertz is the measure used for pitch, or frequency of sound), while dogs can hear up to 40,000 Hz. Cats, though, can hear even higher ones (up to 60,000 Hz), and both pale in comparison to dolphins (up to 100,000 Hz) and bats (up to 120,000 Hz). Dolphins use their incredible hearing range to locate fish—by sending high-pitched squeaks into the water and listening for the echo when it bounces off their prey. Bats are even better at this and can pinpoint a flying moth perfectly even in complete darkness.

That doesn't seem very fair to the moth . . .

Actually, moths can hear sounds of up to 240,000 Hz, so they often hear the bat squeaks coming and dodge out of the way.

Hang on—I thought you said insects were deaf?

Most of them are, but some—including moths, butterflies, grasshoppers, and locusts—have great hearing and use unique sounds to find mates and communicate with each other.

And what about color-blind mammals—is that true? Don't bulls get angry and charge at red things?
No, they don't. Bulls are color-blind, and they charge at the flapping matador's cape because it's a large moving target rather than because it's red. The cape could be green or blue and the bull would still go for it. So the saying "like a red rag to a bull" means nothing—to a bull, it's just a rag.

What about "a bull in a china shop?"
Ah. Still not a good idea.

Can zebras get a striped sunburn?

Under the right conditions, almost any animal can get sunburned, but hair-covered animals like zebras very rarely do. Except on their noses.

Boo. That's no fun. I thought for sure the white stripes would burn . . .
Well, have you ever seen a pink-and-black zebra?

No . . .
There you go, then.

But why don't they burn? I thought pale skin burned easier than dark skin.

The zebra's stripes are made by the coloring of its hairy coat—its skin is actually black underneath. This also answers the question, "Are zebras white with black stripes, or black with white stripes?" quite nicely!

But how does being hairy help? Wouldn't they just get hotter?

Animal hair (including human hair) is made of a protein called keratin, which helps to absorb and reflect the ultraviolet radiation that causes sunburn. That's why it's usually only bald people who get sunburned heads! But zebras don't have hair all over their bodies, and that's why they can still get sunburned noses if they're not careful. To avoid this, they take shelter in the shade at midday, when the Sun is strongest. Most clever animals do this—only human sunbathers are stupid enough to ignore the hot midday sun.

Is that why we get sunburned so often?

Well, it makes sunburn more likely, but you don't have to be out at midday to get it.

Why is sunburn supposed to be so dangerous?

Sunburn itself isn't usually that dangerous, unless your skin gets infected afterward. The dangerous bit is skin cancer. This is caused by ultraviolet (UV) rays from the Sun whacking into the DNA in your skin cells and making new links between bits of DNA that weren't there before. When this happens, the skin cells can go a bit crazy and start multiplying out of control. If you're lucky, they stop this quickly and you get a freckle. If you're unlucky, they may just keep on dividing forever. This can happen if you receive a lot of UV rays to unprotected skin over a long period of time. Fair-haired and red- or ginger-haired people are most at risk, since they generally have fairer skin, but everyone should be careful. The easiest way to avoid it is to wear sunblock, and retreat to the shade once in a while.

Or you could wear a fur coat...
You could, but you'd look a little weird on the beach.

What scares big animals?

It depends where they live and what they've experienced. But it's usually fire, loud noises, and humans—in that order.

So the whole elephant-scared-of-mice thing is...
...funny in cartoons, but complete nonsense, I'm afraid.

So can animals really get scared like we do?
Absolutely. Fear is a natural response to danger, which animals have evolved—just like teeth, claws, and tusks—to protect

themselves. Some fears the animal is born with. We call these instinctive or primal fears, and good examples are fire and animals bigger than they are. Others, an animal can learn from experience. We call these phobias.

What's the point in learning a phobia?

Sometimes these can be useful: A healthy fear of heights, snakes, or spiders can keep a wild animal alive long enough to learn how to deal with them properly. Others can be exaggerated and become harmful to the animal. This happens most often in humans (see the *Top 10 list of common and strange phobias* on page 122), but can also happen in animals. Dogs can develop phobias of random things like hot-air balloons or trash can liners (mine was scared of both!). Big animals are—of course—bigger than most other animals around them, so they're afraid of fewer things. But fire, loud noises, and humans are pretty common fears even for them.

DON'T BE RIDICULOUS!

OK, so I understand the fear of fire, but why loud noises?

Many animals associate loud noises with the crack of thunder, so this may be a primal fear that helps them avoid getting struck by lightning.

And why humans? Why should they be scared if they're bigger than us?

In most places in the world, animals have learned from experience that we're dangerous and have developed a kind of people-phobia. In the past, we hunted them with spears and arrows; nowadays, we have guns. Wherever we have gone in the world, we have destroyed—or almost destroyed—at least one species of animal through hunting. After thousands of years, most animals have us figured out.

Are there any fearless animals?

Interestingly, in the few places we've discovered that stayed untouched by humans for thousands of years—like remote islands or thick, impenetrable jungles—the animals don't seem to fear us, since they've had no reason to. But they still fear other things like fire or loud bangs, so you couldn't call them fearless. Similarly, lions, tigers, and elephants might seem fearless, but really they only attack because they're scared of what we might do to them. Given a choice, most of them stay well away from us, and it's actually quite hard to get close to them as a result.

At the opposite end of the scale, the friendly, flightless dodo became extinct because it lived on the previously unpeopled island of Mauritius, so it wasn't wary enough. When people, pigs, dogs, and rats arrived in the seventeenth century, the people hunted them by simply walking up and clubbing them on the head (until they got bored with it), while the other animal invaders ate their eggs and young. As a result, the dodo became extinct within a hundred years of the newcomers arriving there. So people-phobia seems like quite a healthy fear for an animal to have. We recently discovered an isolated community of animals in a remote area of the Sumatran jungle. Let's hope the animals there figure us out quicker than the dodo did.

Top 10 phobias

(in no particular order)

Acrophobia: fear of heights
Agoraphobia: fear of wide open/crowded places
Achluophobia: fear of the dark
Astraphobia: fear of thunder and lightning
Scolionophobia: fear of school
Ergophobia: fear of work
Lutraphobia: fear of otters
Genuphobia: fear of knees
Xanthophobia: fear of the color (or word) yellow
Panophobia: fear of everything

Why are there no three-legged animals?

Because of the way legs evolved, and how they're used by the animal. Legs always develop in pairs, and animals always have an even number of them. Even when it doesn't look that way.

But wouldn't five legs work just as well as two or four?
Not really. Having an even number of legs means the animal is properly balanced, as the push from a leg (or set of legs) on one side of the body is balanced by a push from the other side. Otherwise, the animal would either have to compensate by pushing less on one side or walk in circles.

Duh. Of course. I knew that. But what if you had two back legs—one on each side—and one front leg in the middle?
Well, that kind of "tripod" shape *could* work, but it doesn't happen in practice because of the way that legs develop in the early animal embryo.

They *always* grow in pairs, then?
Yep. Always.

But why?
Because all animals develop from a single cell—an egg cell that fuses with a sperm cell as it's fertilized, right?

Right.

So that cell divides to make two, each of those new cells divides again to make four, then again to make eight, sixteen, thirty-two, and so on. Before you know it you've got a big ball of cells called a blastocyst. This then folds in on itself several times, and after a bit of messy cellular origami, it develops a head end, a tail end, and left and right sides. Now you've got a basic embryo.

OK...

Next, the embryo develops segments—repeating sections along its length that allow it to make repeating structures like the bones of the neck, spine, and tail (called vertebrae), or pairs of arms and legs. A set of genes, called the Hox genes, tells the embryo how many segments to make and what kind of segment each will be. Four-legged animals develop by repeating the "pair of limbs" segment once, and differences appear between the front and back legs later on (for two-legged animals, the front limbs turn into arms or wings).

For insects, the "limb" segments get repeated three times, giving six legs. For crabs, lobsters, and shrimp, they repeat five times, giving ten legs. For centipedes and millipedes, the segments get repeated between 13 and 380 times, giving them between 26 and 760 legs (not 100 and 1,000, as most people think).

The important thing is: Whatever the animal, and however many legs, they always grow in pairs because of these segments in the embryo.

What about starfish? They can have five legs, can't they?
It looks that way, but in fact, those "legs" are actually arms, or, more accurately, "bits of body." And underneath each one, it has hundreds of tiny tentacle "feet," which it uses to get around. And guess what? There's an even number of them.

Doesn't *anything* have three legs?
Well, there is one thing . . .

What?!
A fly. If you cut it in half, lengthwise.

(Groan.)
Sorry.

Why can't whales and dolphins breathe underwater?

Because they evolved to breathe on land first, and unlike fish they have lungs instead of gills.

So what's the difference between lungs and gills?
Well, they're both used for the same thing: getting oxygen into an animal's bloodstream and getting carbon dioxide out. Both gills and lungs have tiny blood vessels all over them so

that gases (oxygen and carbon dioxide) can be filtered in and dumped out of the blood. The difference is in what goes into them: Gills are water filters while lungs are air filters.

Huh?

Fish gills are basically feathery combs that filter oxygen from water swallowed by the fish as it swims. Lungs are inflatable sacs that fill with air, not water, and gas filtering goes on in the very depths of them—in tiny, berrylike chambers called *alveoli.*

Oh—I get it.

As the fishy ancestors of all mammals (including whales, dolphins, and humans) first made their way on to the shore to feed and breed, they had to evolve lungs so that they could breathe for long periods out of the water. Some of their descendants then reduced (and finally lost) their gills, becoming full-time, permanent, air-breathing animals. Some of these air-breathers then evolved into large land mammals—most of which stayed on dry land. But one family of mammals, the *cetaceans* (dolphins, whales, and porpoises), made their way back to the water. But they kept their lungs.

So dolphins and whales used to live on dry land? How did they get around, then?

It wasn't dolphins and whales but their *ancestors* that lived on dry land. And they walked, like most other things.

What?! With stubby flippers and no legs?!!

No. These ancestor animals *had* legs. They looked a bit like a hippo, only with a long tail and a longer, more pointed snout. (Sounds strange, doesn't it? But we have fossils to prove this is what they looked like.) They didn't evolve flippers—or lose their legs—until they went back to the water.

So why didn't they evolve gills again too?

The simple answer is: because they didn't have to. Evolution doesn't happen because the species wants to do it. Nor because only the fittest, best-adapted animals survive. All that happens is that the weakest or most poorly adapted animals get killed off in each generation.[*]

For the hippolike ancestors of whales and dolphins, flipperlike limbs helped these animals get about and catch fish in the water, so flippered animals tended to survive better than nonflippered ones, and eventually only flippered ones were left. On the other hand, they managed fine with lungs, so it wasn't necessary to evolve gills. Diving to catch fish and surfacing for air seemed to work well enough, so they simply evolved ways of holding their breath underwater so they could stay down for hours rather than minutes.

Is that it? They just couldn't be bothered?

Well, they didn't actually decide, one way or the other—nature did that for them. Plus there's a little bit more to it than

---

[*] See *What's the point of flightless birds?* (page 129) for another example of how this works.

that. To evolve new structures in the body, you need the building blocks there to begin with.

For example, bat wings probably started out as a bit of webbing between the spindly fingers of a mouselike bat ancestor. As the fingers got longer—and the flaps of skin between them larger—they eventually became wings.

But when our amphibian ancestors evolved lungs and reduced their gills, they also lost the bits used to build working gills. (Pieces of the gill eventually evolved into jaw and ear bones—but that's a whole other story!)

After this, it became too difficult to go back, and lungs—even for sea-dwelling creatures—were still the way forward. That's why, even now, they can't actually breathe underwater. And it's also why we're unlikely to evolve into merpeople in the future.

Shame. That'd be cool.
Suppose so. If you like fish or krill for breakfast every day . . .

What's the point of flightless birds?

Flightless birds usually get along fine without being able to fly—they've found other ways to live. So why bother? If they could, they might ask the other birds: What's the point of flying?

Eh? I don't get that. I mean, birds are supposed to fly, aren't they? That's what they're for. I ask you—what kind of bird can't fly? A stupid bird, that's what kind.

Well, even flightless birds *used* to fly once. They just got out of the habit of it when they learned (and evolved) to do other things. These things gave them an advantage over other birds. Even flying ones, believe it or not.

Like what? What could be better than flying?

Stop for a minute and think about penguins. They live in the Antarctic, where it's extremely cold. Almost no animals live there, but those that do have to try to save as much energy as possible so that they can stay warm. Plus, there are no insects, so for a bird there's nothing to eat but fish.

Now, you could spend all your time flapping about and diving into the ocean, trying to catch the odd fish that came near the surface . . . or you could go to where the fish are, by swimming.

Penguins use their wings to "fly" underwater (pretty skillfully too, if you've ever seen them do it), and they do much better at hunting fish than most flying seabirds do catching them. So a penguin might ask, "What's the point in flying?" It also takes far less energy and muscle to use wings for swimming and gliding underwater than it does to stay airborne. And living in the Antarctic, penguins need to save as much energy as they can just to keep warm and survive.

OK, so penguins aren't stupid. But what about emus and ostriches? What about dodos?!

Emus and ostriches have long legs for fast sprinting and do much better at catching food and avoiding predators than you'd think. (They also have a pretty nasty kick.) They live and look a lot like the feathery dinosaurs they evolved from.[*] Dodos were pretty much bigger than most other things where they lived, on the then-remote island of Mauritius.[**] They had no natural predators, so they got by just fine for thousands of years until people arrived, bringing the animals that ate their eggs and drove them to extinction.

Oh. I hadn't thought about it like that. Sad, really.

That's right. Respect for the dodo! Long live the penguin! All hail the kiwi!

You mean there used to be flying fruit too?

(Sigh.) No.

Oh. I knew that.

[*] See *Why are there no dinosaurs any more?* (page 131) for more details.
[**] See *What scares big animals?* (page 119) for more details.

Why are there no dinosaurs any more?

Most of the dinosaurs were wiped out 65 million years ago, probably after a huge meteorite impact destroyed their environment. But there are still some around, if you know where to look for them ...

What?! They're still alive?! Where? Why didn't anyone tell me?!
Hold on—I'll explain everything ...

It's Loch Ness, isn't it? I knew it ...
No. It's not Loch Ness. Or that's extremely unlikely, at the very least. There would have to be a whole family of them, and ...

Where then?
All right, all right—I'll tell you. They're all around you.

But—hang on, I haven't seen ... I mean ... what?!
Let me explain. Like I said, most of the dinosaurs were wiped out around 65 million years ago, at the end of the Cretaceous period of the Earth's history. We think this probably happened when an object hit the Earth—probably landing in Mexico, leaving a

crater over 120 miles across, which we can still see today.* It may have been a comet or maybe just a meteorite, but whatever it was, it was over 6 miles wide and it released as much energy as a million nuclear missiles. This caused earthquakes that shattered mountains, triggered enormous tsunami that pounded into the land and threw enough dust and earth into the air to block out the Sun for more than a year.

Wow! That'd do it.

For most of the dinosaurs, it did. Those that weren't killed in the blast or flooding perished later as their food sources disappeared. As the Sun-starved plants died, so did the big plant eaters that depended on them. The big meat eaters—like tyrannosaurs—ate the big plant eaters, so they soon followed. Besides the dinosaurs, the asteroid probably destroyed over two-thirds of the animal species on the planet. But incredibly, many animals survived, and some did better than ever before in the absence of the dominating dinos. These survivors included our ancestors—small, scavenging mammals more like mice and shrews than the apelike creatures we are today. Along with the early mammals, there were also fish, reptiles, insects . . . and some of the smaller dinosaurs that ate them.

So where are those dinosaurs now?

Well, unfortunately, most of these smaller dinosaurs followed their larger cousins into extinction. We can't be sure why, but it may be that they were simply less well adapted to a chang-

* See Could comets or asteroids really blow up the Earth if they hit us—like in the movies? (page 43) to find out more about this.

ing environment than the mammals and other reptiles they competed with. We know that the global climate changed at around the same time—whether or not the asteroid caused the change, the climate was warmer and milder before it struck and much cooler afterward—so that might be one reason they died off.

In any case, not all of them died. One group—called the *therapods*—survived alongside the other animals and started to evolve into something more familiar. They became birds.

Birds?! Like the little cute flappy things?! You're joking, right?

I'm serious. Scientists noticed the similarities in body shape between birds and small dinosaurs years ago, but until recently they couldn't decide if one had evolved from the other, or if birds and small dinosaurs had evolved the same features separately. Now though, all the evidence points to one evolving from the other. Birds are, in fact, highly evolved therapod dinosaurs. So if you want to see a dinosaur—look up!

Does that mean some dinosaurs had wings, then?

Not at first, no.

What about pterodactyls?

Well, pterodactyls and other pterosaurs aren't really dinosaurs and didn't really evolve into birds at all. Their wings are completely different from birds' wings, and they died out around the same time as the larger dinosaurs.

Some therapod dinosaurs, the ancestors to birds, eventually became able to fly after evolving feathers. Originally, these were probably for keeping warm—only becoming useful for gliding and "assisted jumping" (flapping for height) to catch insects later on. They also lost their teeth and evolved smooth beaks instead. This is all evidenced by the discovery of fossils showing "dino-birds": dinolike animals with feathers and even stubby wings. Also, geneticists can now activate old, dormant "dinosaur genes" in birds like chickens, making them grow sharp teeth within their beaks (and creating scary-looking dino-chickens!).

Awesome! Does that mean we'll be able to make dinosaurs again, like in *Jurassic Park*?
Possibly, one day, yes. We can't get DNA from amber the way they did in the movie, but we may one day be able to recreate a dinosaur genome using supercomputers. If so, it's possible we could then grow a baby dinosaur in an ostrich egg. But this is all just theory at the moment and, at the very least, a long way off.

I'll have a tyrannosaur, please.
I said not yet. And I'd ask your parents first, if I were you . . .

Do spiders have ears?

No, they don't. But this doesn't seem to bother them too much. Probably because they can hear things through their legs. Oh, and they can smell and taste things through their legs too.

What?! That's crazy!

Crazy, but true. Spider legs are one of the most amazing and fascinating things in the entire animal kingdom. Didn't you ever wonder why spider legs were so hairy?

Uh . . . no. But I am wondering now . . .

Well, part of the reason is that the spider uses hairs to "listen" to its surroundings—sensing the sounds and movements made by predators and prey to help avoid danger and catch food.

But what good is hair for hearing with?

Actually, hair is essential for hearing. You use it to hear things too. It's just that the hairs are in your inner ear, behind your eardrum.

Come again?

Sounds are just waves of pressure traveling through molecules of air (or water, metal, or whatever the sound is traveling

through). When something makes a sound in air, what's actually happening is that it's vibrating back and forth, causing waves of air pressure to spread out from it in all directions. These travel through the air to your ears, where they hit the thin membrane of your eardrum, causing that to vibrate too.

OK, I get that. What happens next?

Next, this vibration is transferred through a set of tiny bones behind the eardrum to your cochlea—which looks a bit like a tiny snail shell. The cochlea is filled with fluid, but it is also lined with thousands of tiny hairs, which run along the length of the spiraling, shell-like tube. When the vibration reaches the cochlea, it causes pressure waves in the fluid, which the hairs pick up—like tiny antennae—and turn into an electrical signal sent to the brain. The brain then translates this signal into a specific sound, which we can then recognize from memory as "guitar string," "burp," "helicopter," or whatever.

Cool. But if spiders don't have ears, how do they do it?

Spiders don't have ears, and they don't hear things the same way we do. But they do have thousands of tiny hairs on their legs, called *trichobotria*, which can detect waves of air pressure caused by sounds or sudden movements. So while they might not be able to tell exactly what each sound is, they can certainly tell where it's coming from and whether it's likely to be a threat (like a bird or another spider) or lunch (like a fly).

So that's why spider legs are so hairy?

That's part of the reason. But not all those hairs are used for hearing. Others can detect tiny amounts of chemicals on a surface or in the air using special *chemoreceptors*, like the ones found on your tongue. These hairs are clustered around the tip of the leg, or "foot," so spiders literally taste things by stepping on them. Also on the "foot" is another chemical-sensing organ that can detect odor and humidity. So spiders smell through their feet too.

This is too weird.

Told you it was amazing, didn't I? But there's yet another set of hairs on a spider's foot called *setae*. And this is the best part: Each of these hairs is hairy too, and that's how they stick to walls and climb smooth surfaces.

What?!

Each foot is covered with thousands of setae, and each of these branches into thousands of smaller hairs called *setules*. These are so tiny that you can hardly see them, even with the most powerful microscope in the world. These setules use a special kind of electrical attraction to stick to surfaces—a bit like when you rub a balloon on your head and stick it to the wall using static electricity. But this force only works over tiny distances, so the hair and the surface can't be more than a few nanometers (or billionths of a meter) apart. This is why the setules have to be so incredibly tiny. Even the smooth-est surfaces, on a microscopic scale, look rough. They have microscopic bumps and cracks all over them, and the setules are small enough to fit around and into these shapes, bring-ing them close enough to the surface for the sticky electrical force to kick in.

Cool. But if it sticks so well, how does the spider let go of the wall again?

It rips or peels its foot off the wall—a bit like pulling apart a sticky Velcro fastener. We're only just starting to understand how it all works, but scientists hope they can use this know-ledge to make "sticky" boots for astronauts. These would let them walk around the surface of a spacecraft in orbit without falling off and drifting away into space.

Sweet! I want a pair of those!

You'll have to get behind me—I'll be first in line!

Being Human

Ahh—the human body. Forged over millions of years into a finely tuned machine. Incredibly complex and perfectly adapted to its environment, it has allowed us to become the most powerful and intelligent creatures on the planet.

But if you think about it, being human can be pretty gross at times. For all that we've achieved, we still sneeze, burp, fart, and poop our way through life. Like huge meaty balloons filled to the bursting point with snot, gas, and worse.

And if our bodies are so clever and complex, how come our eyes go blurry underwater? And how come a blob of ice cream—eaten too quickly—can bring us to our knees?

Here we explore the mysteries of brain freeze and more, and find out what it *really* means to be human.

Why is snot green?

Basically, because it's the result of a fight between nasty bugs and body cells that make green-colored goo.

What?!

Seriously. Snot is made of a sticky substance produced inside the nose that traps and flushes out harmful bacteria.* These nasty bugs try to get up your nose when you breathe them in. The sticky stuff stops them from getting down your throat and into your lungs, and it also contains cells that your body produces to fight and kill the bugs. It's these that make the green goo. Sneezing and blowing your nose help to clear it all out.

Ugh. Fine. But what do they make the green goo for?

The body cells form part of the incredibly clever and complex defense system in your body. They make special proteins called *lysozymes,* which help them bust open, eat, and digest the bacteria—a bit like the acid in your stomach. For this reason, we call the cells *phagocytes,* which is Latin for "eaty-cells"

---

* See *What would happen if you sneezed and farted at the same time?* (page 158) for more details about snot.

(which you may prefer, but biologists use "phagocytes" because it sounds smarter and more important). It's one of these bacteria-busting proteins that has the green color.

But why green, and not blue or purple?

This is purely because the protein contains a form of iron that reflects green light and absorbs all the other colors.*
Incidentally, you find a similar protein in wasabi, the type of horseradish you eat with Japanese sushi, which is why that's green too. Think about that next time you eat horseradish. Or a booger.

I don't eat boogers. I don't even pick my nose.

Of course you don't. No one does. No one rolls them up and flicks them, or sticks them under the desk either.

That's right. But if someone did . . . why would the booger change color to dark green, brown, or black?

That's because once it's out of its warm, moist home in your nose, the snot begins to dry up as water from it evaporates into the air. When this happens, the phagocytes die and the greenish proteins within them break up—removing the green color from the booger.

After this, bacteria in the air settle onto the booger and start to eat it (waste not, want not, as my mom always says). They chew up all the bits of phagocyte, dead bacteria, and skin

---

* See What colors can't you see if you're color-blind? (page 146) for an explanation of how this works.

cells found in the snot, until all that's left is a dried-up mass of brownish-black protein leftovers. And even that gets eaten eventually.

Hang on a minute—how did you know boogers change color if you never pick your nose?

Oops.

Top 10 places to stick a booger

1	Under a table
2	Under your chair
3	Under your tongue
4	On the wall
5	On a friend
6	In someone's pencil case
7	In someone's lunch
8	Behind a steering wheel
9	Behind your head
10	Back up your nose again

Why do your eyes go
blurry underwater?

Because our eyes are made to work in
air. If we surround them with water
instead, the light entering the eyes
gets bent too much, and we can't
focus well enough to see clear shapes.

Light gets bent? I thought light traveled in straight lines.
It does. But sometimes, as it moves from one type of material
(like air) into another (like water or glass), it can be *refracted*.
This means the beam of light changes direction slightly as it
enters or exits a different material. So really it's redirected,
rather than bent.

What do you mean?
Think of a glass bottle. When you look through it, things on
the other side can look strange—bigger or longer than they
are when you look straight at them, right?

Right.
Well, this is because when you look straight at an object, beams
of light (usually provided by the Sun or a light bulb) bounce off

it, travel through one material—the air—and go straight into your eyes, where they get focused into a point by the lens inside. But when there's a bottle in the way, the light beams travel from the air into the glass (changing course slightly as they do so), through the air in the bottle (changing course again), then into the glass once more (another course change) and finally back into the air (you guessed it—changing course once more). So maybe it's not so surprising that by the time the pattern of light beams reaches your eye the pattern has changed or shifted. This makes the object behind the bottle look different—magnified or stretched—as a result.

The same thing happens when you look at things underwater from above the surface. Objects on the bottom of a pool or on the seabed look distorted and closer to the surface than they really are because the light rebounding off them gets refracted as it leaves the water and enters the air.

Well, yeah, they look weird, but you can still see them OK. So why do they go blurry when you're underwater?

As human eyes evolved in air, they were fine-tuned for focusing light moving into them from air, not water. When you're underwater, your eye has no air around it. So, unlike the previous examples, the light beams move directly from the water and into your eye, bending like crazy as they do so. Your lenses are unable to focus these properly, so you can't get a clear image of the object you're looking at. Just a blurry one, at best.

So why does wearing goggles help?

Wearing goggles puts a layer of air back between your eyes and the water, so they can focus again. The image you get is still a bit magnified, but it's clear. Unless the goggles fill up with water. Then you're back to where you started.

What about other animals? Do their eyes go blurry underwater too?

For some—like bears and monkeys—yes, they do. Other animals, especially those that spend a lot of time underwater diving for food, have evolved ways around this problem.

Fish, obviously, need to see underwater. But fish eyes are different from ours. They evolved to work underwater, so they can focus and see just fine. (Actually, most of them can't see as clearly as we do, anyway.) Penguins, like most birds, do see very well. But their eyes have flat corneas (outer lenses or "eye windows" that focus light into the eyes) to help reduce the bending of light when they're hunting underwater.

That explains why you never see a penguin with goggles on.

Yes, I guess it does. Because I'd always wondered about that . . .

Me too.

What colors can't you see if you're color-blind?

It could be red, green, blue, or yellow. It depends what kind of color blindness you have, and whether you're a boy or a girl. Even then, it's not that you can't see these colors—it's just that you can't tell the difference between them.

So, if color-blind people can't see red, green, blue, or yellow . . . then what's left? Do they see in black and white?

No, not at all. A few very rare people, called *monochromats,* do see only in shades of gray. But most color-blind people can see most of the colors you can. They just have trouble telling the difference between specific pairs of them.

Which ones?

As I said, it depends which type of color blindness you have. For one type, the most common one, it's the difference between certain reds and greens. For another, it's the difference between some blues and yellows.

But, even then, this doesn't mean they'd see all one color if they looked at, say, a Swedish flag (which is a blue cross on a yellow background). They'd still see a *contrast* or difference

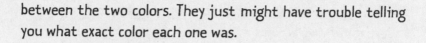

between the two colors. They just might have trouble telling you what exact color each one was.

Weird.

Not really. In fact, even two people with average color vision will often disagree on what color they are looking at. Color perception is quite a subtle thing. For this reason, even if they have a form of color blindness, many people go their whole lives without realizing they have it at all.

So how do you get it?

It's a *genetic condition*, which means you usually inherit it from your parents, rather than catch it or acquire it during your life. (Although, in some rare cases, chemical burns to the eyes have been known to cause color blindness too.) It happens when you inherit a faulty gene—or bit of DNA—from one or both of your parents. This gene normally makes a protein found in the back of your eye called a *cone receptor,* which allows you to translate light beams into brain signals meaning "blue," "red," "yellow," and so on. You have two copies of these genes, so if one of them is faulty, the other one can still make enough receptors for your color vision to be fine. But if both genes are faulty, then you can't make any of that kind of receptor at all, and you end up color-blind.

But why is it different between boys and girls?

Because boys are missing a bit of DNA that only girls have.

Really? That doesn't seem very fair . . .

Let me explain.

147

Genes come in sets called *chromosomes.* Boys and girls both have twenty-three pairs of these, or forty-six chromosomes altogether. In girls, this includes a pair called the X chromosomes. Boys, however, have just one X, paired with another called the Y chromosome. And here's the thing: The X and Y do not make an exact pair like the others. The X and Y are similar but not identical. The Y is shorter than the X and is missing several bits found on the X. And one of these missing bits contains the gene for those all-important red-green receptors we were talking about before.

So girls are better than boys?

Well, for girls, even if one of their X chromosomes has a damaged or faulty receptor gene, they still have a backup copy on the other X. For boys, inheriting a faulty gene on their only X chromosome means they're stuck with it since they don't have a backup.

All this means that while lots of girls carry the gene for red-green color blindness, it's usually only boys that actually suffer from it. Other forms of color blindness, like blue-yellow, are not related to genes on the X or Y chromosomes, so you see them in girls and boys in roughly equal amounts.

But basically what you're saying is girls are better than boys, right?

Not better, just different.

Whatever.

> **If you swallow a burp, does it turn into a fart?**

> Sometimes, yes. Either that, or it simply turns into a (slightly stinkier) burp that comes back up later. As far as the body's concerned, it's "better out than in," I'm afraid.

Does that mean farts and burps are basically the same thing?

In a way, yes. Both are gases released from your digestive system—just from opposite ends. They're made in slightly different ways, though.

Really? So what are farts and burps made of?

Burps are mostly made of oxygen and carbon dioxide, plus a few other gases for aroma. They're made as you swallow air with your food, which makes it as far down as your stomach before being churned back out again a little while later. Farts are a bit more complicated. They contain some swallowed air but also methane, hydrogen sulfide (which provides the "rotten egg" smell), and other gases released both by normal digestion and by bacteria living in your intestines.

Why do you do more burps when you drink soda and more farts when you eat beans?

Carbonated drinks, like soda, contain carbon dioxide, which is added under pressure to give the fizzy bubbles. Drink them down fast and the gases build up in your stomach until they blast their way back up your *esophagus* (or food-tube), out of your mouth, and into the face of a disapproving aunt.

Beans contain lots of cellulose, a fibrous material that is hard for you to digest but is happily broken down by your gut bacteria. In doing so, they produce extra carbon dioxide. This time it goes down instead of up, builds up at the rectum (or bum passage) and finally rattles out at an impressive speed into the waiting world.

Why do they smell and sound so different?

They smell different partly due to their different contents, but also because, frankly, farts spend longer inside you picking up smells before they resurface. They sound different because they move through differently shaped vessels on the way out. Much like a wind or brass instrument, the various twists and turns the gas has to go through before it gets out—plus the force of the initial blast—affects the tone of the sound you get. Burps rattle up the comparatively simple and open tube of your esophagus, past your vocal cords (handy for that burp-talking trick), and out of your mouth and nose. So you get a fairly deep, low tone and a smooth release of air.

Fart noises are much more varied. After making their way to your rectum, the anus (or "bum door") is held shut by a muscle called a *sphincter*. If it seeps out, the fart is silent (but deadly). If it's forced out, you get a vibration of the sphincter muscles, producing an impressive range of different sounds, from low rumble to high squeak. On balance, then, the *bum trumpet* is a much better instrument than the *burpaphone*.

So, if swallowing air means that a burp can turn into a fart, then why not the other way around?

Because the tubes of your digestive system contain safety valves at key points to stop digested food from flowing backward and up to the mouth. This would not only be extremely unpleasant, but could also be painful as, once it clears your stomach, the slurry of food gets quite acidic and can actually burn your esophagus. These valves, also called sphincters, are found at the entrance and exit to your stomach, and at the junction between your small and large intestines. It's your *pyloric sphincter*—the one between your stomach and your intestines that stops fart gas making its way back to the stomach and turning into a burp.

What if the valves didn't work?

Then you'd fart out of your mouth and down your nose. I don't know about you, but I think I prefer the current arrangement . . .

Why does your poop go runny when you get diarrhea?

All poop starts out looking like diarrhea. But your body usually dries it out in the final lap through your guts. It's when your guts get upset that the world falls out of your bottom . . .

Gross! So your body dries out the poop to stop it just falling out of your bottom?

Well, not really. The purpose of digestion isn't to make a nice dry poop—it's to get as many useful nutrients and as much water as possible out of all the stuff you eat and drink. Poop is just what's left after all this extraction is done. If it goes right, then the poop comes out fairly solid, as most of the water has been taken out of it and kept inside the body. If it goes wrong, then the water stays in the poop . . . and you have trouble keeping the poop in at all.

Does all that happen in your stomach?

No, not at all. Most people think food is digested in your stomach, then just passes through a lot of long tubes to your bottom, but this isn't really how it works at all. Your stomach does digest things a little, but it's mostly just a bag for storing food so you can eat more of it at once. That way, you can eat just two or three big meals a day rather than having to nibble and munch small quantities all day long—as many animals do.

How does it work, then?

Digestion actually starts in your mouth as your teeth physically mash up the food and, with added spit (or *saliva*) supplied by your *salivary glands*, turns it into a squishy ball (or *bolus*). Saliva also contains special proteins (or *enzymes*), which start to break down starchy foods into sugars.

This small, easy-to-digest ball is then swallowed and squeezed down your food-tube to your stomach. There the food (along with all the water you drink) is collected and gets churned and mashed even more by the squeezing of muscles in the walls of your stomach. It also breaks up a bit more as strong acids in your stomach start to dissolve it into a slurry called *chyme*. (If you interrupt digestion at this point by throwing up, then this is the stuff you see coming out.)

But if you think about it, all you've done so far is liquify the food by putting it through a kind of body-blender—a meaty mashing machine with acids in it. You haven't actually digested it by absorbing the food or water into your body yet.

So where does that happen?

In the final two parts of your digestive system—the small and large intestines. The *small intestine* is a narrow tube over 20 feet long (it's actually a lot longer than the large intestine—it's called "small" because it's thinner). It works like a nutrient sponge, using the millions of tiny, spongy fingers that line it to draw essential sugars, proteins, fats, and salts out of the poo-slurry as it passes through. These nutrients are then filtered through your liver and transported around your body in your bloodstream.

The large intestine is more like a water sponge. Again, it has millions of tiny, spongy fingers (called villi) lining it, and it's these that absorb water from the poop, drying it out. The water is then filtered through your kidneys, from there most of it is passed to your blood and body cells, and the rest is passed to your bladder to be peed away along with any extra salts.

So how does it go wrong?

When the villi of the intestines get attacked by bacteria, viruses, or other nasty *microbes* you take in with sketchy food or water, they lose the ability to absorb and hold water. So the poop stays wet and runny, and the whole lot comes out, with interesting effects ranging from "dribble" to "lawn sprinkler."

Yuck! How can you stop it?

By not letting your guts get infected in the first place. This means being careful not to eat food that has been stored too long or that hasn't been heated well enough to kill the microbes inside. Water is usually fine, as drinking water is filtered to remove some of these and we get used to other microbes. But we can sometimes get diarrhea on vacation—when we're traveling abroad—when we're not used to the local water. So it's best to drink bottled water abroad.

What about once you've got it—how do you stop it then?
You don't. You just have to let it "run" its course. Any attempt to plug it could end with dangerous poop pressure building up inside your body, possibly turning you into a poo-powered rocket if you did it for long enough. But you'd probably just get very ill, so it's best to just set up camp on the toilet and drink water and nutrients to replace the stuff you lose. And next time, try to avoid the iffy hotdogs.

Why do other people yawn after you do?

This is a tricky one. Lots of animals yawn, but only humans and chimps find it contagious. It's not to get more oxygen, as we used to believe. The best guess so far is that it's a signal telling you and others in your group to stop and take a rest.

What? But yawning is, like, automatic, isn't it? You don't do it to tell people you're tired.
Well, it is an automatic action, or *reflex*, but not in the same way as blinking or pulling your hand away from a scalding-hot

object. These are both reflexes that evolved to protect you—one from getting things in your eye, the other from getting burned. Yawning happens much slower after it's triggered, and you have more control over whether you do it or not. Plus you don't blink and jump away from a hot object just because you see someone else do it.

But you yawn when you're tired, so doesn't it just mean you need sleep?

Yes, it does. But while other animals also yawn when they get tired, most of them don't find yawning contagious. In fact, chimpanzees are the only other animals we've seen do this. Even humans don't start doing it until they're about two years old.

So what does that mean?

Well, chimps are the only other animals we know that can recognize and understand both their own and another animal's state of mind—something we call *empathy*. This may not be so surprising, since they are our closest living relatives in the animal world. Human infants don't show real empathy until they reach two years old because the parts of the brain that allow them to react in this way haven't yet developed.

So what all this probably means is that while yawning evolved as a signal to yourself that you need sleep, contagious yawning is something else—a signal that generates empathy in others. In other words, when you yawn, others will see you and—without realizing it—imagine how tired you are feeling. If they're even a bit tired too, they'll yawn back, and everyone else around can see you're both tired. This might end in a chain reaction, with everyone around you yawning, one after the other!

But what use is that?

We're not sure yet, but it may be that this allows a group of people (or chimps) to weigh how tired the whole group is and decide whether or not to keep moving or take a rest. This makes sure that no one is left behind, and also that everyone's ready to run or defend themselves in an emergency. So contagious yawning may have evolved as a way to keep a group together and well rested. Both of these help to keep everyone in the group safe.

Are there any other group signals like this?

Smiling, laughing, frowning, and crying can also be contagious, but again, only in chimps and humans over a certain age. So it could be that smiling and laughing tell others in the group "I'm happy" or "I'm fine—don't worry about me." On the flipside, frowning and crying could tell the group "I'm not happy" or "I need some attention."

Do humans and chimps copy each other like this?

Well, what did you do last time you saw a laughing chimp?

What would happen if you sneezed and farted at the same time?

As farts and sneezes come from separate sources, humans can (and do) sneeze and fart simultaneously. This saves us from the nightmare of sneeze-fart implosion.

What are sneezes for, anyway?

They're quick blasts of air from the lungs, used to clear out things that irritate or try to infect your airways, like dust and bacteria.

But sneezes come from your throat, don't they? At least it feels like they do . . .

They come *through* your throat at high pressure, so that's why you can feel them there so strongly. But they actually start in your lungs. The sudden rush of air, which can come out at over 100 mph, is made by quickly contracting the muscles of the throat and ribs, and by the diaphragm (a sheet of muscle found under your lungs) contracting and relaxing. This both narrows your throat and forces a lot of air through it at once, which blasts out loads of snot (mucus) lining your throat, mouth, and nose.

How did the snot get there in the first place?

You made it on purpose. Or rather, your body did to trap bacteria, dust, pollen, and other stuff you inhale. This is to stop them from getting down into your lungs, where they can interfere with your breathing and infect or damage your lungs. The mucus is made by special cells lining your *trachea* (or windpipe) and throat, called *goblet cells*. They squeeze out a sticky goo that covers the nasties, and the whole lump is shifted upwards by millions of wafting hairs called *cilia*. These hairs that line your throat (unless you're *dumb* enough to burn them off by smoking) work like a conveyor belt—driving the lumps of mucus up to the back of the nose and mouth, where they can be swallowed or blown out. Sneezing is a reflex that helps to clear the mucus out quickly when it starts to block and irritate your airways.

I heard that you can't sneeze with your eyes open. Is that true?

Yes, it is. Try as you might, you just can't do it. Your eyes close as a reflex (or automatically) when the rest of your face muscles tense up to help create the sneeze. But it may also work to stop bacteria and viruses from reentering your body. Once out of the mouth, your sneeze spreads out in the air into millions of tiny droplets called an *aerosol*. Each droplet still contains the bacteria and viruses you're trying to get rid of, so your eyelids close to stop stray droplets from reentering your body through your eyes. This also explains why you should cover your mouth when you sneeze or cough, since you don't want your droplets flying into someone else's face either.

So if air came out of one end with a sneeze and the other with a fart . . . why wouldn't you collapse in the middle?
Because farts and sneezes come from different tubes, and there's plenty of air left in both, even after you do them. Farts come from the *digestive tract,* which runs from your mouth to your bottom, via the stomach and intestines. Sneezes come from your *respiratory tract,* which runs from your mouth and nose to your lungs. This runs alongside the food-tube (or esophagus) in your throat. So the tubes taking air and food into your body are separate, and synchronized sneeze-farting is quite safe.

What about burp-farting?
Also quite safe. So is talk-farting, for that matter. This can be quite useful if you want to cover up the sound of a fart and simply blame the smell on a nearby pet.

Ha-ha. I must try that.
Just try to look surprised, and make sure the cat or dog is nearby before you do it.

Why do you feel hot when you have a cold?

Because your body turns up the heat on purpose to help fight off the germs. After all, it's a virus—not cold weather—that causes the cold in the first place.

Don't you catch a cold because you "catch a chill"?

Not really. If you think about it, plenty of people complain of "summer colds," and you can get cold all the time in the winter without necessarily coming down with a cold.

But you do get them more often in winter, so how do you explain that?

"Catching a cold" results from a combination of dropping your body temperature and inhaling or swallowing droplets of water containing certain types of virus. The main ones that cause colds are called *adenoviruses* and *rhinoviruses*. In winter, the cold weather can cause your core body temperature to drop if you don't wrap up in warm clothes. This makes you less able to fight off infection, but you still have to get the viruses from somewhere in the first place.

So where do they come from?

Well, the other thing that happens in cold weather is that people cluster together indoors more often than they do in summer. This gives more chances for the viruses to spread as you breathe in virus-laden water droplets that are sneezed, coughed, or simply breathed out by other people. Once these droplets are breathed in, the germs settle in the lining of your nose, throat, or lungs and start to multiply. Your immune system can usually fight them off after a day or two, and all you get is a bit tired and snotty.* But some nastier viruses (especially the ones that make it to your lungs) can last for weeks and make you very ill.

So how does getting hotter help?

Getting hotter, or developing a *fever,* is one of your body's

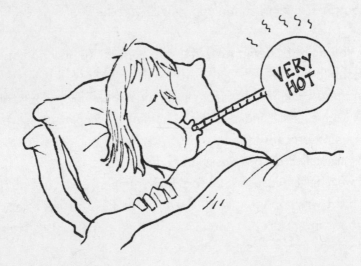

---

* See *What would happen if you sneezed and farted at the same time?* (page 158) for an explanation of how snot works.

natural responses to infection. This is because the kind of bacteria and viruses that infect us have evolved over millions of years to work best at the normal human body temperature of 98.6°F. The proteins they use to make copies of themselves only work at this temperature. Raise the temperature by just one or two degrees and these proteins unfold and break apart, and the bacteria or virus stops multiplying and dies.

So fevers are healthy?

Well, usually they're a sign of infection by viruses or bacteria, but also that the body is trying to fight them off. So generally speaking, you should let them do their thing rather than try to cool off with ice packs or wet towels. Problems only come if they go on too long, or your body temperature gets so high that your body's own proteins stop working too. This happens at body temperatures of 104°F or over, but this hardly ever occurs with colds, only with nastier diseases like pneumonia.

So if colds make you hot, why call them "colds"?

That probably started when people associated them with cold weather. Plus you can't tell someone you have the "hots," or they might think you like them!

What about "the snots?"

Well, that certainly is more descriptive ...

If we evolved from chimps and gorillas, why are there chimps and gorillas?

First of all, we didn't evolve from chimps and gorillas—we just share some great-great-great-great-grandparents with them. Secondly, chimps and gorillas are doing fine as they are (at least for now), so why should they need to evolve any more?

But I'm sure I saw it in a book! There was this chimp, and then a caveman, and then a guy with a beard . . .

Unfortunately, that's not quite how it works. Many books show evolution like this—as if it's a race won by humans, or a ladder with humans at the top. But it's really not.

Why not?

Because if it was a race, then we didn't win, and if it was a ladder, then chimps and gorillas are standing at the top with us. We all evolved from a common ancestor, but we didn't *replace* chimps and gorillas. In fact, we evolved alongside them.

Huh? I don't get it.

Try this. Imagine there's a huge line of people doing that silly "conga" dance where everyone holds on to the hips of the person in front. Now imagine you're at the front and behind you is your dad. Behind your dad is his father (or your grandfather), and behind him is his father, and so on.

OK...

Now, as you go back down the line, you'd see your ancestors trail back into time, until eventually you'd get to "cavemen," or early humans like *homo erectus, homo habilis,* and others. They'd be a bit shorter and hairier than your dad and grandfather, with more sticky-out facial features, but otherwise not too different. Some way behind them would be something that looked a bit (but not exactly) like a chimpanzee. He'd be short, hairy, and would walk using both his feet and the knuckles of his hands (at least he would if he wasn't already doing the conga). How far do you think the line would stretch between you and this creature?

I don't know. Thousands of miles? Millions?

Only about 300 miles.

No way!

Yep, only about 300 miles between you and the ancestor we share with chimpanzees. But it wasn't actually a chimp. It was the animal that—if he started a second conga line by holding on to his other son—would eventually lead to a modern chimp. If the two lines conga'd side-by-side and you walked along them from the back to the front, then dancers level with each other would look more and more different as you went up the line. Until, eventually, you'd arrive at your dad and a chimp waiting side-by-side at the front of the lines.

So evolution is more like a pair of ladders, then?

It's more like thousands of ladders—one for each species alive today. But since they all join up at the bottom (with another shared ancestor further back), it's probably easier to think of evolution like a huge tree, with the first living thing at the base or trunk, and thousands of branches leading to everything alive today. Or a single river that splits into thousands of smaller streams. If you think of it like this, then some streams—like those that lead to tyrannosaurs and dodos—dry up into the earth, while others survive and flow into the future.

So we still have gorillas and chimps because ...

... because they, we, and all the other species alive today have survived the test of time. Whereas tyrannosaurs and dodos have not.

Shame.

Yes, it is. But then again, there wouldn't be many people around if the world were full of tyrannosaurs!

Why are some belly buttons "innies" and others "outies?"

Because a belly button, or *umbilicus*, as it's properly called, is really a scar formed from your lopped-off umbilical cord. Depending on how the scar heals up, you get either a cavity ("innie") or a projection ("outie").

So what does the umbilical cord do?

It's useless after you're born but, while you're in the womb, it's a lifeline to your mother. A *fetus* (or unborn baby) in the womb can't eat, drink, or breathe while it's inside the mother's body. So the umbilical cord contains a blood vessel that transports nutrients and oxygen from the mother's bloodstream to the baby's.

So it connects you to your mother?

Yes, but not directly. It connects you to a branching bag of blood vessels called the *placenta*, which sits alongside the fetus in the womb. The placenta is structured a bit like two trees with interlocking branches. One "trunk" leads to and from the mother's bloodstream. The other trunk is the umbilical cord, which leads to and from the baby's bloodstream. Both trunks lead to branches that overlap and interlock in the middle, forming a tangle of small vessels—the placenta. Nutrients and oxygen move through the walls of these vessels, but the blood supplies stay separate.

So what happens when you're born?

When you're born, you come out first, followed by the placenta. Within a few seconds, you start using your lungs to breathe and, soon after, you'll be drinking milk for nutrients—so you don't need the umbilical cord any more. Doctors usually put a clamp on it to squeeze it shut (but even if they don't, it closes up by itself pretty quickly anyway), and it shrivels up and falls off after a few days. All that's left is a scar on your belly where the cord once was—a lump of flesh that can form either inside or outside the body. This gives either an "innie" or an "outie" belly button or *navel*.

If it's a scar, why doesn't it just heal over?

It does, it just doesn't heal over perfectly flat. If not enough cord remains outside the skin (as is often the case), the remaining cord is sucked beneath the surface of the skin and fuses to the wall of the abdominal cavity beneath. This is the space where your guts, kidneys, and many other organs sit.

So how deep does it go and where does it lead to?

Well, the navel is separated from the abdominal cavity by a few layers of skin, so an "innie" belly button is less than an inch deep. But behind that wall are the remains of the umbilical vein leading to your liver, which also closes and shrivels into a thin fiber soon after you're born.

Why don't other animals have belly buttons?

Actually, most mammals do—including cats, dogs, monkeys, dolphins, and whales! It's just that they're not so obvious if they're covered with hair or fur, or otherwise hidden from view.

All right, then. The big question is: Where does belly-button fluff come from?

From your clothes. Fluff or lint forms as small fibers from your clothing are left in the navel and gather into bigger lumps. Interestingly, boys normally have more than girls (they have hairier belly buttons, which helps to collect fluff), and it's often different colors too. Boys' fluff is usually blue, black, or brown, while girls' fluff can be white, yellow, purple, or pink!

This is because girls tend to wear more varied colors, while boys stick with a few.

. . . and if you unscrew your belly button, does your butt fall off?

No. That's just plain crazy.

Sorry. Must have heard that one at school . . .

> ## Are people with bigger heads smarter?

> No. They just have bigger heads. Even bigger brains don't mean smarter people, as some "cavemen" had bigger brains than us. It's how you use your brain that counts.

But if you have a big head, you have a big brain, right?
No, not necessarily. The size of your head, as measured from the outside, depends mostly on how the bones of your skull develop as you grow up. That doesn't mean your skull is packed to the brim with gray matter, though. Your brain is quite a bit smaller than your skull, and it sits inside layers of fluid and a set of membranes called *meninges,* which vary in thickness. So you could have a big head, lots of fluid, and a regular or smallish brain.

OK, but let's say you do have a bigger brain. That has to mean you're smarter, right? I mean, we've got bigger brains than other animals, and we're smarter than them . . .
It's true that humans do have pretty big brains relative to the size of their bodies. And it's also true that animals with larger brains (like dogs and dolphins) tend to be more intelligent than, say, mice or insects, which have tiny ones.

Aha! Got you! So I'm right, then! Bigger brains *are* better!
Not exactly.

Why not?

Because there are plenty of exceptions to this rule. Whales and elephants, for example, have brains over six times bigger than ours. This is because bigger brains also go hand-in-hand with bigger bodies, as they're needed for proper control and movement (rather than whale poetry and elephant chess). This may also be why Neanderthal "cavemen," relatives of the early humans we evolved from, had bigger brains than us too. And we wouldn't say they were smarter than us either.

If the brain were simple, like a muscle, then bigger would mean smarter, just as bigger muscles are often stronger ones. But the brain isn't simple. It's incredibly complex. In fact, we still don't understand how most of it works, but we know enough to figure out why bigger brains don't always make smart people.

So why is that?

It's because "cleverness" and "intelligence" depend more on how the brain is wired than they do on sheer size. The average brain weighs about 3 pounds—about the same as a bag of sugar or a bunch of bananas—and contains about 100 billion nerve cells or *neurons*. These neurons are clustered together in regions, some of which receive information about the rest of the body (*sensory neurons*) while others send information to the body (*motor neurons*). Another type (*inter neurons*) connects to one another and to sensory and motor neurons within the brain, and it's these connections that allow the more complex functions of reasoning, memory, and intelligent thought.

In particular, it's the neurons of one area of the brain—the *cerebral cortex*—that seem to provide us with what we call intelligence. It's the cortex that makes us smart. Humans and other smart animals are clever not simply because their brains are bigger, but because their cortex regions are better developed. But even then, having the best equipment won't make you any better if you don't actually use it.

What do you mean?

Intelligence is partly something you're born with, but also something you learn. Your brain doesn't stay the same for your whole life. Whenever you learn something new, your brain reshapes itself and grows new connections between neurons. Because of this, children become smarter every day simply by using their brains to understand the world around them. Adults can continue to learn throughout their lives. How clever they become will largely depend on how much they try to learn.

So I could be a genius one day?

Absolutely. Just keep on learnin' . . .

Why do we walk on two legs (instead of four)?

To be honest—we don't know for sure. Our ancestors may have started the habit to help gather food, to defend themselves, or even to wade across rivers!

We really don't know?
Well, there are lots of theories about why we walk on two legs, but none has been accepted as the one right answer to the question.

I heard we did it so we could use tools and carry things . . .
There you go, you see. There's a problem right there.

What's that?
Well, using tools is certainly easier if you stand on two legs. And walking on two legs—rather than four—does free up your hands so it's easier to carry stuff . . .

So what's the problem?
The problem is, while this explains the advantages of standing and walking upright, evolution doesn't work like that. An animal can't look ahead in time and think, *I should start walking*

upright! That would totally free up my hands for other stuff, like tools, and spears, and cell phones, and PlayStation, and . . .

OK, OK—I get the idea.

Right. You can't evolve on purpose. Once our ancestors had evolved an upright stance or posture, they found out that walking upright lets you do all sorts of useful things, like use tools and weapons. But they needed a reason to stand up in the first place—one that meant the difference between life and death. So that only the ones that did it survived better or had more offspring than the ones that didn't. That's how evolution works. By filtering out the bad rather than helping the good to get better.

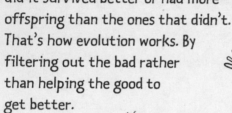

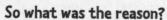

So what was the reason?

Like I said, there have been lots of ideas, but no one knows for sure which is correct. "So they could use tools and weapons" was the oldest idea, but most people now doubt this for the reasons above. The next theory was "so they could carry food." But many people now doubt this too, since chimps, gorillas, and monkeys seem to manage this well enough walking on all fours (using three limbs to walk and one to hold the food).

Next came the idea that we started walking upright so we could see farther ahead. Since it was thought our ancestors evolved in Africa,[*] and Africa is covered in plains of long grass (or *savannahs*), then walking upright would have lifted our heads over the thick grasses, helping us to spot mates or dangerous predators from farther away.

That seems to make sense . . .

Yes, it does. Until you consider that Africa wasn't always dry and covered in long grasses. In fact, when our ancestors first started walking upright, it was much wetter and covered in forests, lakes, and rivers. This led to another idea—perhaps we didn't start walking upright at all. Maybe we started *wading* upright instead, and only started walking on dry land later on.

What?!

I'm serious. Chimpanzees (our closest living animal relatives) walk upright sometimes too. But they do it only about 6% of the time when they're on dry land. Give them a stream or pool to walk into and they *always* wade in on two legs, 100% of the time. It's easy to imagine how this habit would have helped our ancestors survive. They often would have had to cross rivers and streams to escape predators or to reach new food sources.

Couldn't they do that on all fours?

Not really, no. "Wading on all fours" is otherwise known as "drowning," since it usually leaves your mouth and nose

---

[*] See *Why do people from different countries look different from each other?* (page 176).

underwater. So only those skilled at two-legged, upright wading survived. Over time, their hips and spines would have evolved to support this habit, and at some point they just kept on walking onto dry land. That's when the advantages of walking upright—like carrying food, tools, and weapons—could kick in.

So we're all just weird wading apes?
That's about the gist of it, yes.

Why do people from different countries look different from each other?

Actually, people from different countries look pretty much the same. The differences that do exist—like skin color and eye shape—are due to where our ancestors lived, and how they spread out from Africa and across the world.

But people do look different. And it seems like the farther away they live from each other, the more different they look, right?

Well—sometimes, I guess. It's true that Chinese and Korean people look more similar to each other than, say, Chinese and African people do. But it's not where people live that makes them different.

What d'you mean?

Imagine this. Let's say I lined three average-looking white kids up next to each other, like a police line-up—an American, an Australian, and a South African. Assuming I didn't let them talk, could you pick out which one was which?

Probably not.

Right. And they're from three different continents.

But that's cheating. They could all look the same because their families all came from the same part of Europe.

OK. So maybe it's not where you live now, but where your ancestors come from, that makes you look different. Those three guys might look the same because their ancestors were all average-looking white Europeans.

All right, then—why do white Europeans, Chinese people, and Africans all look different from each other?

Ahh—now we're getting somewhere. Good question. The short answer is this: Their ancestors all started out in Africa, looking like Africans. But as they split off into groups and traveled across the globe, the descendants of the Chinese and Europeans gradually changed in appearance as they adapted to their new homes.

I don't get it.

Well, the only real difference between white Europeans and black Africans is their skin color. Years ago, average-looking, white European scientists used to tell us that this was because Africans started out perfectly white (like them), but were tanned black by the Sun. But they had it completely the wrong way around—in fact, those very same scientists (or rather, their ancestors) started out with black skin and became pasty as they moved northward out of their homeland in Africa. This, it turns out, is due to vitamins.

What, those things you eat to stay healthy?

Yes, kind of. Vitamins are things your body needs to stay healthy, and we usually get them through food (and, more recently, pills). But your body can also make some vitamins for itself. Your skin can make vitamin D, which is important for healthy bones and teeth, but it needs plenty of sunlight to do so. In sunny regions, black skin lets through just enough sunlight to make vitamin D while also blocking the parts of sunlight that cause skin cancer. But in less sunny areas farther north (or south),* black skin blocks too much sun to allow vitamin D to be made properly. So the black African ancestors of white Europeans got pastier as they moved out of Africa and settled farther north.

---

* See *If countries are hotter in the south, why doesn't the South Pole melt?* (page 92) if you don't quite follow this.

So what about Chinese people and African people? Why do they look so different from each other?
Well, the ancestors of the Chinese and other Asian people also became paler as they moved northward (and eastward) out of Africa, for the same reason. The only other notable difference between Africans, Europeans, and Asians is the shape of their eyes and eyelids. Asians tend to have more almond-shaped eyes, and have an extra fold of skin (called an *epicanthal fold*) on their eyelids. It is thought that this narrowing and shielding of the eyes evolved to help protect the ancient settlers of Asia from the blinding effects of the snows and winds of the mountains and plains. Some of them then passed this trait on to their Inuit and American Indian descendants, who crossed the land bridge from Asia to North America thousands of years ago.

Is that it? We're all the same?
Yes.

And the only reason people look different at all is because of a bit of weather and a vitamin?
Exactly.

Kind of makes you wonder why we didn't figure all that out sooner.
Yep. It certainly does.

Why do you get "brain freeze" when you eat ice cream too fast?

"Brain freeze" or "ice-cream headache" happens when cold food chills the roof of your mouth, irritating nerves there and causing blood vessels in your brain to temporarily close up.

Whoa! That sounds dangerous!

Don't worry, it's not. For most people the effect only lasts a few seconds, and the blood vessels soon open up again, stopping the pain. It's all pretty harmless and temporary.

Why does it happen?

Basically because we didn't evolve to eat frozen food. Ice cream can only be made by chilling the ingredients (milk, cream, sugar, and fruit or flavorings) artificially, using freezers or chemicals kept at very low temperatures.

Chemicals? Is that safe?

Yes, and it's quite common. Actually, some of the best ice creams in the world are made by freezing the ingredients in seconds rather than hours, using liquid nitrogen. This is kept at an amazingly cold −321°F and is simply poured onto the mix of ingredients. All the heat from the ingredients rushes into the chilled nitrogen, and the milk, cream, and sugar freeze in seconds, giving delicious, instant ice cream!

So ice cream hurts us because it's unnaturally cold?

In a way, yes. Our bodies weren't made for it. But it's fine as long as you don't eat it too fast. As soon as you put it in your mouth, the ice cream starts to heat up to match your body temperature (around 98.6°F), so it doesn't stay very cold for long.

Unless you chug a whole scoop at once?

Exactly. With a mouth full of it, the heat will move out of your body and into the ice cream before it has time to melt. When the roof of your mouth (or *palate*) loses heat in this way, the effect causes nerves within to fire off signals to the brain, telling the blood vessels above to contract. This causes a shift in blood pressure in the brain, and often results in a painful headache in the mid-frontal region, right behind the eyes.

How do you stop it?

It usually goes away on its own within ten seconds or so; as the ice cream melts (or is swallowed), your palate heats up again, and the nerves and vessels return to normal. If you want to speed it up, you can hold your tongue against the roof of your mouth or quickly drink some warm water. Either one will help heat the palate faster.

But the simplest way to stop it is . . .

I know—don't get it in the first place, right?

Exactly. Just eat your ice cream and drink your cold drinks a little slower, and you have no reason to "fear the freeze."

What are scabs for, and is it OK to pick them?

Scabs put a lid on your cuts and scrapes, keeping blood in and nasty bacteria out. And, although it may be fun, picking your scabs is dangerous.

You mean if you pick a scab you could bleed to death?!
No, not likely. Most scabs form over cuts too small to bleed that much. Cuts and scrapes that big usually need stitches or skin grafts.

So why is it dangerous to pick them?
Because scabs are like temporary Band-Aids that cover your cuts until the skin has a chance to grow back underneath. They fall off on their own when the repairs are complete. Pick them off any sooner, and you risk opening up the wound again. At best, this will mean you just form another scab, so the wound takes longer to heal than it would have. But the second scab may be even bigger than the first and is more likely to leave a permanent scar on your skin when it finally comes off.

At worst, the wound could become infected and lead to much bigger problems.

Like what? What's the big deal about a little cut?

Ordinarily, nothing. This is because your body has a strong immune system and a clever system of blood clotting to prevent too much blood loss from the cut. When you get cut, the cells nearby release signals that start two major chain reactions. One chain reaction brings immune cells to the area to fight off any bacteria trying to get in through the cut. These are white blood cells that drift around in your bloodstream waiting for an attack. Some of them, called *macrophages,* can punch holes in the bacteria or eat them whole and digest them with acids. Others, called *B-Cells,* make special proteins called *antibodies,* which surround the bacteria. These either kill the bacteria themselves or act as sticky warning labels so that nearby white *helper cells* can recognize them and summon *killer cells* to destroy the invader.

So why do we get scabs?

Scabs are made of the bits left over from this battle—the dead bacteria and immune cells—plus a special stringy protein called *fibrin.* Fibrin is the end result of the other chain reaction—the one that leads to a blood clot. Again, when the wound occurs, special blood cells (this time called *platelets*) stick together and react with other proteins called *clotting factors* to build a clot. This clot is made from fibrin, which stretches across the wound, pulls the edges together, and plugs the gap between them. This helps to stop any more blood from escaping and also stops bacteria from getting in.

What happens if bacteria do get in?

It depends on what type of bacteria. Some of them we can fight off easily enough, and the wound heals normally. Others, like the clostridium bacteria that cause gas gangrene, can dodge the immune system long enough to do serious damage. So you could end up losing an entire leg or arm from one infected cut! Worse still, if bacteria make it into the bloodstream, they can travel around the body to other organs like your liver, heart, or brain, doing damage there instead. And you *really* don't want that to happen.

Yikes! I'm never picking a scab again!

If you're healthy, and you keep the cut clean, none of this should be a problem. But the scab is there for a reason, and it'll fall off on its own when it's ready. Until then, just enjoy it. Admire the colors, impress your friends . . . but leave it alone!

Fantastic Futures

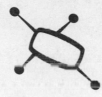

What will life be like in the future?

Will we come home from work or school to watch 3D movies on TV?

Will we listen to music and talk to friends on MP3 players and cell phones so tiny that they fit behind our eardrums?

Perhaps we won't even go to school or to work. Perhaps there will be robots to do all the work for us. Maybe people will slowly turn into robots as they replace their limbs and organs with tougher and stronger robotic body parts.

How will we get around? Will our cars be able to fly? Could we build machines to teleport us from place to place, or even backward and forward in time?

And how will we power all these gadgets, machines, and robots? Will we still have enough electricity to go around? Can we make everything solar powered? What if we can't?

We can't know for sure what the future will be like. But some parts of it—it seems—are here already . . .

Will evil computers and robots take over the world?

Maybe—but there doesn't seem to be any danger of it yet. Even the most advanced computers and robots around today are bits of junk compared to human brains and bodies.

But computers and robots are getting more powerful all the time, aren't they?

Yes, they are. In fact, over the last fifty years the technology has been developing so fast that computers have been doubling in power roughly every eighteen months. We call this doubling rule *Moore's Law,* after computer scientist Gordon Moore—the guy who first noticed it was happening. Robots too have progressed pretty quickly. In 1738, we had the first mechanical duck (which could eat grain, flap its wings, and poop). Today we have ASIMO—a complex, humanlike robot built by Honda that can walk unassisted on two legs (even up and down stairs!) and recognize human faces and voices.

So sooner or later, they'll end up more powerful than us, right? Then it's *Terminator* time!! The robots will be out to get us, and they'll build big flying things, and . . .

Whoa! Slow down there. While it is possible that this could

happen, it doesn't look very likely at the moment. So there's no need to panic.

Why not?

Well, for starters—despite what Moore's Law says—computers probably won't continue developing this fast for long. It might be that, since Moore's Law was pointed out, computer developers have been using it as a goal.

So we're only getting computers twice as powerful every eighteen months because we're trying to?

Exactly. And there may come a point where we fail to meet that goal.

Aside from that, even if computer power is doubling every eighteen months, that doesn't mean we're putting all that extra power to use. How we use computers depends on how we program them—they can't do anything we don't tell them to do—and programs (or bits of software, like iTunes or Internet Explorer) aren't developing at the same speed as the computers they run on. Fifty years ago, scientists thought it wouldn't be long until computers could understand spoken English and we could just talk to them to give instructions. Fifty years later, computers still can't handle spoken language, and we're still using keyboards. So there's no danger of a computer superbrain outwitting us at the moment.

What about robots?

Again, even the most advanced robots around today, like ASIMO, are still pretty simple and clumsy compared to us. ASIMO can walk (and even jog) like we do. But if he gave you any trouble, a gentle shove would tip him over and leave him unable to get up again. So today's robots are closer to toasters than Terminators.

But some day they could make one that moves as fast as us, or even faster, right?

True. There will probably be humanlike robots (or *androids*) that are stronger than us too. But they still wouldn't be dangerous unless they learned to think for themselves. The word robot comes from the Czech word *robota,* which means "slave." And that's what they are—slaves. Hopefully, by the time real *artificial intelligence* (or AI) is created,[*] we'll have figured out a way to keep robots under control with special "safety" programs or circuits. These would force robots to follow rules or laws that would stop them from ever harming humans. The science-fiction writer Isaac Asimov (whom ASIMO was named after) created the idea of "Laws of Robotics" over sixty years ago for one of his stories. But since we're still some way off from making truly intelligent robots, we won't be needing these Asimov circuits any time soon.

So we're fine for now, then?

Yes, I'd say there's very little chance of being held hostage by an elevator or strangled by your iPod just yet.

Argh! Don't say that! Now I'll worry about it!

(Sigh.)

---

[*] See *Will computers ever be smarter than people?* (page 190) for more about this.

Asimov's 3 Laws of Robotics

First Law: A robot may not injure a human being, or, through inaction, allow a human being to come to harm.

Second Law: A robot must obey orders given to it by humans, except where such orders would conflict with the First Law.

Third Law: A robot must protect its own existence as long as such protection does not conflict with the First or Second Law.

Will computers ever be smarter than people?

Difficult to say, but it probably depends on what you mean by "smart." Many computers today can already "think" faster and better than people, but only in very limited ways. For now, at least, computers are not very intelligent or smart by our standards. In the future—who knows?

But I thought some computers could beat people at chess and stuff. Doesn't that mean they're pretty smart already?

That's true. A particularly powerful computer called Deep Blue beat the world champion Garry Kasparov in a chess match in May 1997. But that only worked because winning at chess is ultimately based on how many moves ahead you can "see" (or predict the results of) to decide the best moves. Using raw computer power, Deep Blue could predict possible moves up to twelve moves ahead. Even the best chess players, like Kasparov, can only predict up to about ten moves ahead.

WHY IS SNOT GREEN? •

So the computer was smarter, then?

Not really. All that game proved was that a computer could store and handle more bits of information about chess moves than a human brain can. But being good at a board game isn't a real measure of "intelligence." Even if it was, there are other games that computers are pretty hopeless at. For example, in the more complex Japanese board game Go, even the most advanced computers can't beat novice players. The same goes for complex card games like poker, which computers are no good at because they can't bluff (or even cheat) the way human players do.

Why not?

Because with games like these, using calculations alone won't work. To play good poker or Go, you need other things like intuition, creativity, and even empathy—which is the ability to imagine how someone is feeling. Simple as they are, games like these help to demonstrate why information processing is not the same as intelligence, and why even the most powerful calculators can't be called "smart." At least not yet.

So what makes us so much better than them?

In short, our brains. The average human brain weighs about 3 pounds—about the same as a bunch of bananas!—but contains about 100 billion *neurons,* or *nerve cells.* In computer terms, it uses these to store about 100 million MB (megabytes) of information, which it can handle at a speed of over 100 million MIPS (million computer instructions per second). While some of the most advanced computers around today may just be able to top this, it's not speed or memory power but complexity and flexibility that give us the edge.

We're not entirely sure how it all works yet, but we know that each neuron in the brain connects to an average of 1,000 others, and that this creates over 1 quadrillion connections. That's a big number. If you tried to write it, it'd be a one with twenty-four zeros after it! It's this vast number of connections that makes the brain so powerful. It allows us to go beyond simple calculations and into the realms of emotion and *consciousness*—or thinking for ourselves. Until computers can be made truly conscious, we won't really have created true artificial intelligence (AI). Judging by what we have now, we still have a long way to go.

How will we know when we've done it?
Well, for one thing, it'll pass the basic test that all computers so far have failed.

What test?
The Turing Test. This was created in 1950 by Alan Turing, one of the scientists involved in building the first modern computers. He said that the real test of artificial intelligence was this: If a person talked (through a keyboard and computer screen) with another person and a computer, and couldn't tell

which was which . . . then you'd have created a truly intelligent computer. No computer has yet passed this test.

That's what you think.
Eh?

402*Error* insufficient memory/640K barrier exceeded%$↑
Argh!!!! All this time I've been talking to a computer?!

Ha-ha. Gotcha.
Grrrrr.

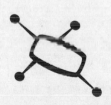

Could athletes make themselves better at sports with robot arms and legs?

For some sports, like running, yes. For most other sports, no—not really. Not unless they replaced the rest of their bodies too, and that would seem a bit unfair. Robot limbs might be stronger and faster than real ones, but they still rely on the fleshy bits they're attached to.

Hang on a mo'. Robot arms and legs are stronger than human ones, right?
Some of them are, yes.

So an athlete with robot arms or legs would definitely beat someone without them, right?
Not necessarily. In fact—probably not. For most sports, *cyborgs* (humans with robot limbs) wouldn't be any better off than normal athletes at all.

I don't get it.
OK—give me an example. What would your cyborg win at?

Soccer. With robot legs, it could kick super-shots no goalie could save. Or tennis. With robot arms, it could hit a killer serve . . .
But to win those games you also need reflexes, timing, and coordination. These depend on your brain, not just your arms and legs.

All right, then—what about the high jump? Surely you could win that with super-springy robot legs?
Unfortunately, robot legs—at least the ones we have today—tend to be much heavier than fleshy ones, so probably not. Even if we make super-light, super-powerful legs in the future, using them to do a super-jump could injure you. This is because the jumping motion depends not only on your leg muscles, but also on the bits your legs are attached to, like the muscles of your hips and spine. Pulling on these too hard with your robot legs could break your pelvis or damage your spinal column.

Fine. Weightlifters with robot arms, then.
The same problem could apply, I'm afraid. Lifting uses muscles in your legs as well as your arms. So even if your arms could handle the super-heavy weight, that doesn't mean your fleshy legs wouldn't buckle underneath it.

Gahh!!! What about with robot arms *and* legs?
No good either, as that still leaves the bit in the middle. During a lift, the weight is transferred from your arms down to your legs through the muscles and bones of your spine. A super-heavy weight could still snap your spine (or the spinal muscles,

at least) when you tried to lift it. You could, of course, just replace your whole body with robot parts. But then is it really you competing any more? Go down that route and athletics would become more like motor racing—where the best machines often win races rather than the best drivers.

Not nearly so much fun to watch.

Boo!! Boring!! So robot body parts are no good for sports?

Well, there are some sports where high-tech artificial limbs could be an advantage. Running, in particular, depends on little else but the raw power in the legs and the length of the runner's stride. In tests, some disabled runners have broken track records using artificial "running legs." These attach below the knee, are shaped much like kangaroo feet, and are made of a springy material that allows the runner to almost "bounce" with each stride—the spring absorbing and returning some of the energy that the runner puts into each leg.

This might suggest that while today's controllable "robot" limbs—which are basically high-tech copies of human limbs—don't seem to fare so well in sports, that doesn't mean they never will. Maybe we'll develop new designs based on animal legs—or even wheels and tracks, like cars and tanks! And while the "robot" body parts we have now might not be any good for sports, they do have some other, more worthwhile, uses.

Like what?

If you think about it, we already have cyborgs living among us. Electromechanical body parts (or *prosthetics*) have been around for a while now in the form of hearing aids, pacemakers, and even artificial hearts, and plenty of people have them. Hearing aids used to be earpieces attached to big boxes that you wore hanging around your neck. Now, hard-of-hearing people can have tiny digital implants inserted behind their eardrums.

Similarly, medical scientists are already testing tiny eye implants connected to video cameras, giving us the hope of "artificial eyes" for the blind. It could be that one day, many or most of us will have some kind of cyborg body part like this.

You mean like Darth Vader in *Star Wars?*

Er ... kind of, yes. Let's hope it turns out better for us than him.

> **Will we just teleport from place to place in the future?**

> Believe it or not, scientists have managed to "teleport" some things already. But as for "beaming up," *Star Trek*–style, either there's no hope at all ... or we're a very long way off.

What do you mean "we've done it already"? When? Where?

In 1998, a group of physicists at the California Institute of Technology successfully teleported a photon (or a particle of light) over a distance of 3 feet. Then in 2004, an Australian group topped that by teleporting a whole stream of photons, in the form of a laser beam, from one side of their laboratory to the other.

Really? How did they do that?

They did it using pairs of particles, through a strange process called "quantum entanglement." Basically, two photons were "entangled" so that they shared the same information, then one of them was sent through a cable to another point. Then they used a laser to change the information on one of the photons, which was copied (or teleported) to the other one immediately—due to the spooky entanglement effect. Finally, they destroyed the original photon, leaving only the copy behind. So at the end of it all, the original photon was gone and an exact copy existed in another place. *Voilà*—teleported particle.

Pah. That doesn't sound much like teleporting to me. That just sounds like copying something and getting rid of the original one. That's cheating, isn't it?

Well, if you think about it, that's all you're really doing when you teleport something. To "beam" something from one place to another you have to turn the solid matter of the particle (paper clip, person, or whatever) into information. Then you send that information to a destination—by sending it down an electrical cable or transmitting it in the form of electromagnetic waves. When the signal is received, the information is used to create an exact copy at the other end. So now it's both *here* and *there*, and to complete the process you destroy the original object so it isn't here any more—it's *there* instead. Get it?

Would that really work?

In theory—yes, it would. At the moment, teleporting solid objects (rather than beams of light) around seems highly unlikely. But the experts say that even if we can't do it now, teleporting an atom is theoretically possible. From there we could progress to groups of atoms, and on to whole objects made of atoms, like paper clips. That said, many scientists doubt that we'll ever get that far. They say that this "teleporting particle" effect might only ever be useful for new kinds of computing and communication technology.

OK, but if we could do solid objects, would it work on a person?

Probably not, for two big reasons. The first one is that there's just too much information in the human body.

What do you mean?

Solid objects are made of atoms, and in order to copy or tele-port an entire object, you would first have to get all the in-

HE WAS HERE A SECOND AGO!

formation about every atom in the object. A typical steel paper clip contains about one thousand billion trillion iron and carbon atoms, ordered into a simple cagelike formation. The human body, however, contains around seven thousand trillion trillion atoms—seven billion times more than a paper clip. What's more, there are many more types of atoms (including hydrogen, oxygen, calcium, sulfur, and many others), and they're arranged in infinitely more complex ways than the simple, repeating cagelike structure of the paper clip.

Take all this into account, and you have to see that trying to measure every bit of information about all of these atoms would be practically impossible. Get it wrong, and you'd end up with your leg sticking out of your head or your organs inside out. That's the first reason why teleportation wouldn't work on people.

So what's the other reason?
The second reason is that the "destroy the old copy" bit of teleportation would tend to, er . . . kill you.

That's no good.
No, it's not. I think I'd rather take the bus.

Will people have flying cars?

Several types of flying cars already exist, but right now they're too noisy, expensive, and dangerous to use. So if they're to become more popular in the future, we'll have to make them quieter, cheaper, and much safer— none of which will be easy.

We already have them? What do they look like?

Well, there are a few different kinds. First, there is the "wheeled helicopter" type, like the AirScooter—which you steer around with a pair of handlebars, like you find on a bike. It can fly at 55 mph for over two hours and go up to 10,000 feet above sea level. If that doesn't sound cool enough for you, there's the Urban-X, which lifts off using huge, downward-facing fans on either side of its futuristic-looking cockpit. Then there's the Skycar, which looks more like a jet fighter and has four movable engines—two on each side. All three of these can take off and land vertically, without a runway.

Then there's the convertible car/plane type. These look much like normal cars on the road, but they can be converted for use as aircraft by unfolding their wings and tailfins, and moving power from the wheels to propellers or rotors.

Cool! So why is no one driving—I mean, flying—them already?

Well, for one thing, a shiny new Skycar will set you back about one million dollars. So most people just can't afford one.

Rich people, then. Like Bill Gates and Madonna.

Because most of them are still being tested and, for one reason or another, none of them has yet been found suitable or safe to use as personal transports. The helicopter-based models are often ruled out because the spinning rotors are thought to be too dangerous for regular people to use around their homes. (I guess they figure that sooner or later, somebody will forget to duck as they get in, and things could get really messy!) Other models may be too unreliable or too dangerous to be made legal. And even the ones that are considered safe enough are too noisy and cause too much pollution to use in and around crowded towns and cities. So right now, even rich celebrities aren't allowed to fly them.

Won't they make them safer, cheaper, cleaner, and quieter in future?

Most probably, yes—but you'd still have a problem jumping into one and taking it for a spin, since you'd need a full pilot's license to fly one. Think about it—a car flying through the air isn't really a car any more—it's an aircraft. To fly an aircraft safely, you have to learn how to take off, land, and generally move around in three dimensions (left/ right, forward/backward, and up/

down) rather than the two you need to drive a car (no up/down to worry about there). Otherwise you could end up flying into power lines on takeoff, or crash landing on somebody's house.

OK, OK. So I'll get a pilot's license. *Now* can I have one?

Well, you can . . . but there's still a good chance you'll crash it before long.

Why's that? I bet I'd be an ace car-pilot . . .

Maybe so, but you've still got the problem of air-traffic control. Just because you know how to fly your car-o-plane and you know where you want to go, doesn't mean you'll be the only one in the sky. Even if you stay clear of airports and fly only at low altitudes to avoid airplanes, there are still helicopters to worry about. And just imagine if everybody else had a Skycar or Urban-X too. There would be thousands of them crisscrossing the sky at once, like a cloud of huge metal insects. Even the best pilots couldn't avoid a midair crash for long in conditions like these.

Boo. So we'll never have flying cars, then?

I didn't say that. It's just that we'll probably need a "sky traffic" system before we can start flying them all over the place. And that will need a bit more time to develop. Before we all leave the roads for the skies, we'll have to make sure the skies are properly organized.

How would that work?

What we'd need is a system of "skyways," or 3D roads in the sky. These probably wouldn't be real, visible roads like the ones we have on the ground—it's rather tricky painting white dotted lines in the sky! Instead, they might be virtual tubes or tunnels projected onto the pilot's windscreen or helmet visor.* Perhaps a bit like the 3D computer graphics fighter pilots use to target enemy planes. The pilot would then follow these virtual paths through the sky, taking safe routes up and back down again to the final destination—staying clear of other traffic all the way. Flying-car traffic would then crisscross the sky in lines rather than in chaos.

Another option could be to turn over control of your car-o-plane to a traffic navigation computer and fly everywhere on autopilot. NASA has actually already started to develop a system like this, called HITS, or Highway In The Sky.

No way! What kind of fun would that be?!

Yeah—I see your point. If you had a flying car, you would prefer to fly it yourself, wouldn't you? But don't worry—HITS would let you take over the controls if you wanted to. Just make sure you don't fall asleep at the wheel!

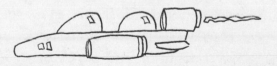

---

* These types of image aren't around yet, but we may not be too far off creating them. See *Will we have real 3D movies, TV, and video games some day soon?* (page 209) for details.

Will we be able to travel back in time?

Some scientists say time travel is impossible. Others say it's possible, but only forward. Still others say you could go backward too—but only a little bit. Either way, we haven't seen any *chrononauts* yet . . .

Why do they think it's impossible?
Well, there are theories that seem to say it's possible—like Einstein's special theory of relativity—but that we will never actually do it, for other reasons. Then there are the general arguments, based on logic or common sense.

What do you mean?
About 100 years ago, Einstein first described the link between space, time, and the speed of light with his special theory of relativity. This basically tells us that time isn't a constant thing—it can change with motion. The faster you go, the more time slows down. So if you were to do a round-trip to a distant galaxy and back, at close to the speed of light, you would only feel the passing of a few years, while thousands of years may have passed on Earth. So in effect, you have traveled thousands of years into the Earth's future.

So that's going forward—what about going back in time?

The special theory of relativity also says that if you could travel faster than light, then traveling or sending messages backward in time might be possible too. Unfortunately, it also says that it would take an impossibly huge amount of energy to speed something up to go faster than the speed of light. Most scientists take this to mean that faster-than-light travel is impossible to achieve. So if we can't do that, then we can't travel back in time either. Of course, there may be other ways to do it. Some physicists have suggested that we might be able to use black holes or wormholes in space to go from one point to another, or even one time to another.* The theories get pretty crazy when you try to work this out, but it seems possible, at least, that this could happen.

So maybe time travel *is* possible, then? It's just that we haven't figured out how to do it yet...

Probably not.

Eh? Why not?

Because if we do figure it out one day, we'd have seen it already.

What?! That doesn't make any sense!!

I know. Time travel really messes with your head. And your grammar.

Look at it this way—if someone in the future invents a

---

* See *What is a black hole , and what would happen if you fell into one?* (page 39) to find out about these.

time machine and people start traveling back in time ... then we'd probably have met some of them already. If *chrononauts* (like astronauts, only they travel in time rather than space) had made it back to our time, then they'd be here right now. And there's no evidence of that. So either time travel is impossible, or it's possible, but you can only go forward. Or backward a bit ... but not as far as our time.

Gahhh!!! That's mental!

It gets worse. What if you went back in time and killed your own parents (either accidentally or on purpose)? Then you would no longer exist. But if you didn't exist, then you couldn't have traveled back in time and killed them in the first place.

Stop it!! This is mashing my brain!!

That's because it's a situation that contradicts itself—a paradox. It seems like it should work, but it doesn't—it's impossible. Because of problems like this, many scientists say time travel is just not possible. It defies logic. But then so do lots of other things that scientists *do* believe, like how electrons get entangled or exist in many places at once, and ...

Enough! No more!

OK, fine. We'll talk about that later. Or maybe earlier ...

NNNNYYYAAAAAAAA!!!

> ## Will we have real 3D movies, TV, and video games some day soon?

> Almost certainly, yes. But it's too early to say how long it'll take, or how good it'll be. Based on what we've made already, though, we could be in for a treat in the near future.

Don't we already have holograms and other 3D stuff?

Kind of, but the 3D stuff we have is not very sophisticated. *Holograms*—flat pictures that appear to be three-dimensional—have been around since 1947. But in the six decades since, no one has been able to turn them into a projected moving image for use in 3D movies. We do have 3D movies, of course. But almost all of them are just 2D screen projections that use polarized glasses (or the same red–green glasses they used in the 1950s) to give the illusion of a 3D image. Some are more convincing than others, but none of them are what scientists and engineers would call perfect 3D.

What about 3D TV?

That's been a long time coming too. Soon after color televisions replaced the first black-and-white ones, people were saying that 3D TVs couldn't be far behind. Sadly, though, no one has quite managed to build one in the four or five decades since. But there may be some hope on the horizon.

How's that?

After years of waiting, and many failed attempts to design and build them, scientists now think that the first three-dimensional holographic TVs may be less than a decade away. A team of engineers in the United States say they have found a way of projecting a moving 3D holographic image through layers of LCD (liquid crystal display) screens. They hope to use this to build a TV set like an open box filled front to back with LCD screens. The hologram would be projected through them from behind, and you'd sit in front, enjoying a basketball game where the ball would seem to bounce around inside the box for real.

Wicked. Looking forward to that. But what about video games? We already have virtual-reality games, right?

Well, like "3D," it depends what you mean by "virtual reality." At the moment, even the most advanced VR games aren't enough to fool us into thinking we're actually *in* the game. The graphics lack textures and lighting effects, and they scroll around in a jerky way, ruining the impression that you're looking at something real. While there might be sights and sounds, there are no smells. And the big problem is you can't touch anything—or, at least, you can't reach out and feel the things you're looking at between your fingers. All this stops you from becoming totally immersed in the game and its virtual environment. Which is the true goal of VR.

So what would real VR look like?

You'd be better off asking "what would real VR *feel* like" since that's the big difference—feel. In true VR, not only would the virtual world around you be almost photo-realistic, but you'd also be able to touch and grab things. Some VR kits are already trying to simulate touch by using special gloves along with the standard VR goggles or visors that show the images. These gloves contain small pressure pads or pins that press against your skin to simulate the sensation of touching—something engineers call *haptic feedback*. The idea is that when you reach out for an object in the game, you feel like you're really touching its surface because the glove is pushing back against your hand as you squeeze it closed. But these haptic feedback devices are still very primitive, and they don't feel at all realistic yet. Better ones may follow in coming years.

So real VR would have to be perfect? Like an exact copy of what you see in real life?

Not at all. In fact, that might be impossible to achieve, even with the most powerful computer systems and graphics.

It would just need to be good enough to fool your brain into thinking it was real. Like an optical illusion, but all around you, and engaging all five of your senses.

Wouldn't that be a bit weird and scary?

Maybe. But would that stop you from trying it?

No way!

Thought not.

Will computers, cell phones, and MP3 players get even smaller?

Almost certainly, yes. Computers may one day fit into a dot on your clothing. Music players and cell phones may fit right inside your ear. Maybe you'll wear a wristwatch that contains all three. All we need first is a "small" change in technology.

Cool! Do you really think all that could happen?
Definitely. Look at how far we've come already. In the 1940s, a computer would have filled a good-sized room. By the 1960s, you could fit one onto a desk, and by the end of the 1980s, most schools and offices had "personal" computers on desks. By the year 2000, we had laptops and palmtops and cell phones that made the ones from the 1990s look like house bricks.

So if we've gone from "room" to "palm" in the last sixty years, who knows how much smaller computers will get over the next sixty? Maybe we'll have "thumbtops," or computers like tiny dots—so small we can hardly see them.

So why can't we just make them that small now?
Actually we can, and we have. IBM has built a simple computer circuit that measures less than twenty nanometers (or thou-

sandths of a millimeter) across. Technically, it's the world's smallest computer. On its own, it's not useful for very much, but it does show that we're on the verge of building computers on a seriously tiny scale. As we learn more about how to create and assemble circuits out of parts the size of atoms (or even using atoms themselves), we'll be pretty much free to make computers as small as we like.

That said, we're still limited at the moment by our interfaces. These are the things like computer keyboards and mice, which let us interact with electronic devices. That's one of the reasons why we don't generally make computers any smaller than a palmtop. If it were any smaller, how would you type into it?

What about if you could just talk to it?

That would be one way around the problem. But we haven't managed to write a program that can recognize natural human speech just yet. Another way could be to use a "projected keyboard." This is an image of a keyboard that is projected from a tiny digital device on to a handy flat surface—like a desk or wall. The device would then use infrared sensors to detect your fingers tapping the virtual "keys," allowing you to set modes, program, or send messages, even if the device itself is smaller than one of your fingers. When we figure out ways to use all these technologies, things will get really interesting . . .

Like how? What kind of things will we get?

Who can say? Some scientists predict that computers will become so small and so cheap to produce that you'll have hundreds or thousands of nanocomputers stitched into your clothes. These wearable computers could monitor your heart rate and hormone levels, sensing your emotions and helping you to deal with everyday situations by making helpful suggestions. Like telling you to take a rest, or which way to go to find a friend, a fast-food place, or a restroom.

I don't know—that sounds a bit creepy to me. How would they talk to you, anyway?

Maybe through a communication device on your wrist, which would be like a cell phone, an MP3 player, a digital video camera, and an Internet browser—all in one. Eventually, this might even have a holographic display,* projecting a 3D image a couple of inches tall into the space above your wrist.

That sounds pretty cool. So you would talk and listen to music using your wrist too? That might look a bit funny . . .

Maybe. Or maybe your nano-cell-MP3 would be so small that you could wear it in your ear. Not just the headphones—the whole thing. Tiny microphones would pick up the vibrations of your voice through your skull, so you'd never have to "pick up" the phone to answer it—you'd just start talking. And your voice-activated MP3 player could be discreetly pumping your favorite tunes into your ear (or maybe both ears) all day long. If the whole thing was hooked up to computers in clothes, your friends could talk to you through the ear implants too.

---

* These types of images aren't around yet, but we may not be far from creating them. See *Will we have real 3D films, TV, and video games some day soon?* (page 209) for details.

Whoa! Now that *is* creepy. Like voices in your head . . .

. . . or the screen image for your Internet browser could be transmitted to special sunglasses or contact lenses. Messages and information from the computers would float before your eyes, pointing out places, people, or products you might be interested in.

Oh, great—so now I'm seeing things too?! You know what? Thanks—but no thanks. I'll stick with my PC and iPod for now.

Suit yourself. But trust me—in the future, this stuff is going to be huge. Or rather—very, very tiny.

Will everything be solar powered?

Not unless we can find a better way of harnessing energy from the Sun. The big problem with solar-power generation is that it doesn't work at night, so you have to store your energy somehow. But if we can figure it out, we'll have a clean, safe, and almost unlimited supply of energy for our daily lives.

But don't we have solar-powered machines already? Like watches and calculators?
Yes, but they're only small gadgets and devices, and they don't need very much energy to run. You don't need to store much energy to keep a watch going in the dark.

Can't we just make the solar batteries bigger for cars and houses and stuff?
We can, and we have. For example, you can now get solar panels for the roof of your house to power your heating and lighting. Every year in Australia there's a solar-powered car race for budding engineers. But these "solar racers" are much smaller

and lighter than normal cars, and they can't hold more than one person. Generally speaking, solar power is really not so good for powering big, energy-hungry machines like regular car, bus, and train engines.

So why doesn't it work?

Well, it works, but not efficiently enough to produce the large amount of energy needed—all at once—to power a large, heavy machine or vehicle. You can store the electricity in batteries, of course. But you can't really charge them as fast as you run them down.

Why not?

Partly because the solar cells used to convert energy from the Sun into electricity aren't very efficient—they only trap and convert about 15% of the energy from the rays of sunlight that hit them. This might be enough if it was sunny all the time—but it isn't. Many countries just don't get enough sunshine to make solar power practical, and even in very sunny places, sunlight gets blocked or absorbed when it's cloudy. And—of course—there's no sunlight to be had when it's nighttime in your part of the world. (The poles get sun for months at a time, but it's dark there for months at a time too.) This means you have to store the electricity somehow, so you can use it later on or somewhere else. More energy is lost as you convert and store it in another form—like in the chemical energy of a battery. So in the end, you simply can't get as much energy as you need.

It's worthless, then. We can't use it.

I didn't say that. You can use it to power lots of things—just not everything. You can power most of the things in your house with a roof covered in solar panels. But if you want an uninterrupted supply of electricity, you still need a back-up energy supply from another source—like a power grid fed by a nuclear or conventional (coal or oil-burning) power plant. Maybe one day we'll figure out a way of gathering energy from the sunlit half of the world during daylight hours and feeding it into a worldwide grid to supply the other half—the one shrouded in night. Until then, we're stuck with small grids supplying local areas only—all fed by coal, oil, and nuclear power sources.

Which kind of defeats the point. Right?

Right. But even nowadays, you can still use solar energy to supplement or add to your regular power supply. And if you use solar power in combination with, say, electricity generated from a windmill, you could still have an environmentally friendly house.

But that still leaves the problem of cars and planes . . .

So what we need is another way of using solar power. Rather than plaster everything with solar cells, what we really need is an efficient way of using solar energy to create another high-energy fuel—like hydrogen. Then we could have clean, hydrogen-powered cars, trains, and aircraft that produce water vapor instead of dirty exhaust fumes, and we'd have the chance of making everything solar powered indirectly via hydrogen fuel.

Would that really be possible?
Absolutely. Look at it like this—in a way, everything on the planet is solar powered already. You, me, cats, dogs, trees, mushrooms, cars, planes—you name it.

Eh? How's that?
Well, it's like this. Our bodies get their energy from food—using water and oxygen to get the energy out and store it in our bodies until we need it. But let's say we ate a hamburger—where did the food get its energy?

Er . . . the cow?
Exactly. The cow extracted and stored energy from the big clumps of grass it ate before it became a burger. Now where did the grass get its energy?

The Sun?
Bingo! The grass uses energy from the Sun to grow. So this means humans, other animals, grasses, and other plants all get their energy from the Sun. Then we use that energy to build cars and planes, to build batteries to power appliances, and to drill for oil to make the fuel we need to power them. Plus, the oil got its energy from the billions of dead plants and animals that were crushed together underground to make it in the first place. So in a way, our vehicles are solar powered already!

Wow. I hadn't thought about it like that before.
That's what science is all about, dude!

Will we ever run out of electricity?

Maybe—maybe not. We can probably keep making electricity for as long as we need it, but it's how we make it that's the problem. There's not much use in having lights and electronic gadgets if we destroy the planet when we use them.

So we can just keep making electricity forever? Then why are we always told that we need to save energy?

Because whether or not we run out of electricity depends on two things: how much we use and how much we produce. Most of us don't have much control over how much (or how) electricity is produced, but we can control how much we use.

That said, most of us are already using quite a lot more than we were thirty or forty years ago and, as technology develops and plays a bigger role in our lives, we'll probably use even more in the future.

So won't it all eventually run out?

Well, let's think about it for a minute. Where does your electricity come from?

Uh . . . the plug.
Right. And before that?

Those power lines outside.
And before that?

Er . . . a power plant somewhere.
And what happens there?

**Well . . . they burn stuff, or use nuclear stuff . . . and
smoke comes out . . . and they make electricity.**
Right. More or less. The stuff they burn is usually natural gas,
coal, or oil. They burn it to heat up huge vats of water to make
steam. Then the steam turns a series of turbines (which look
like big propellers or electric-fan blades), which are connected
to a generator. There, the motion of the spinning turbines
gets transformed into electricity. If it's a nuclear power plant,
then the heat released by two chunks of nuclear fuel when
you place them together is used to boil the water instead.
From there, you get steam, spinning turbines, and electricity
in pretty much the same way.

    The problem is that coal, oil, and gas supplies are gradually
running out, and burning so much of them is probably adding
to the greenhouse effect, which causes global warming.* And
while nuclear fuels can probably provide all the electricity we
need, the nuclear waste they leave behind could damage the
environment.

* See *Is the Earth really getting hotter, and is that so bad?* (page 88) for more about this.

But what about solar power and wind power? Couldn't we use those instead?

You're right—solar and wind power are not only safer for the environment, but also potentially limitless; it's unlikely that we'll ever run out of wind or sunlight. But they do depend on windy and sunny days and, in general, neither of these methods alone could produce and store enough energy to meet all of our needs.* That said, there are other kinds of renewable sources of energy—like wave, tidal, and hydropower—and we do need to use these if we are to keep producing electricity once the coal, oil, and gas are gone. Especially if we don't want to use nuclear.

So what's the answer? Which one is best?

No single method is best—the real solution is probably for each country to use a combination of energy-producing methods best suited to its climate and its energy needs. The United States, for example, could use wind, wave, solar, and hydro-electricity, while sunny African countries might get by on solar alone.

But for the time being, we'll probably have to go on using nuclear and gas-fired power plants until the technology for renewable energy can be improved since, right now, we probably couldn't meet our energy needs with solar and wind power.

---

* See *Will everything be solar powered?* (page 216) to find out about the problems of solar and wind power.

Not even with a million windmills and solar panels?
Well, possibly. But then they would cost a lot of money (and still more energy!) to make, and not everybody wants one on or near their house. We all have to decide for ourselves, I guess.

I'm going to live in a cave and use no electricity at all.
Hey—it worked for our caveman ancestors. But then, they didn't have PlayStation ...

> ## Will policemen and soldiers have laser guns?

> Possibly. Laser weapons have been made already, but they're not cheap, reliable, or portable enough yet to be used. Interestingly, lasers could turn out to be safer than traditional guns. But in the end, the only safe kind of gun is no gun at all . . .

We already have laser guns? Like in the movies?

Well, not really. In the movies, laser "ray guns" zap people (and more often than not, terrifying aliens) with bolts of laser light that fly like bullets. In real life, this is impossible—the *photons* (or particles of light) in a laser beam travel at the speed of light, which is so quick that you can't see it as movement at all. So a laser beam, as we see it, is either "on" or "off." It either makes one unbroken line from the laser to the target or nothing at all. But it never moves in dots, dashes, or bolts.

OK, OK, but you can still fry people with them, right?

Actually, most of the lasers we use every day aren't very dangerous at all, unless they hit you in the eye. Even "cutting" lasers like those used in laser surgery only work over very short distances and wouldn't be very useful as a long-range weapon. Lasers are used *with* guns—to project dots onto the target, improving the shooter's aim. But as yet, none have been used as guns for firing at people through the air.

Why not?

Because there are several problems with making something like that. The first one is power. Lasers convert electricity into strongly focused beams of light—but they aren't very efficient at doing it. This means they require lots of power, which means huge batteries. Then there's overheating. Again, because lasers aren't very efficient, much of the power supplied to them is wasted as heat rather than converted to light. This means you have to cool them down to prevent overheating, which in turn means bulky electric fans or cooling systems. Taken together, huge battery plus huge cooling unit equals massive laser unit. You could make one small enough to mount on a vehicle, but it would be way too heavy to carry in your hands.

OK, fine. But that means you could still make big jeep-mounted ones for frying tanks and stuff with, right?

You could, but you probably couldn't build one powerful enough to "fry" a tank. Even if you could, you'd probably have to be right next to the tank to use it (a slightly dangerous tactic, I think). This is due to yet another problem with lasers, called *blooming*.

Blooming?

Blooming is when a laser loses energy to the air, causing it to lose focus on the target. Basically, this is because the laser beam doesn't just heat the target—it also heats the air around it. This turns the air into a plasma (or super-heated gas), and the more air the beam has to go through, the more energy it loses. So after a few yards and a few seconds, the laser is no good.

But you said some laser weapons have been made. So what *do* we have?

One laser weapon still in testing is the electrolaser. This is small and light enough to be carried as a backpack. The electrolaser takes advantage of the blooming effect rather than avoiding it. It first shoots a laser beam through the air to create a band of plasma leading to the target. Then it sends a powerful electric current through the plasma (which conducts electricity much better than normal air), zapping it with an electric shock. There's also the Active Denial System, which is a vehicle-mounted crowd-frier used to break up riots. But this isn't really a laser at all—it emits microwaves, which heat up the water in the skin, causing painful blistering and swelling. Both these weapons can be adjusted to give either gentle (itchy skin, gentle shock) or severe (serious burns and shocks) effects.

Is that why you said they might be safer than guns?

Yes—not safe, maybe, but safer. Conventional guns are basically portable, handheld cannons. They fire lumps of heavy material, usually lead, which rip into or through a target. There's no adjusting that—you can't set bullets for "stun."

So it would be better if we all had laser guns?

It would be better if we didn't have guns at all. But given the choice, I think I'd rather be zapped than shot. At least until they make lasers more dangerous!

Will we live on the Moon and on other planets?

Living on the Moon is possible, but with no air, no food, and no water, it would take a lot of effort. Other planets might have air and water—or we could even make air and water on them—but we'd have to get there first. So while you could live on other planets, you'd have to ask yourself: Is it worth the trouble?

Why is it so difficult?

Well, the problem is that humans can't live just anywhere, and most places are no good for us—Mars and the Moon included.

Why not?

Because life on Earth has spent the last 4.5 billion years adapting to survive on this particular planet. So take the results (the plants, animals, or people) somewhere that's not Earth, and the chances are we'll have problems.

What kind of problems?

Let me give you a few examples. Our flimsy bodies evolved under the pressure of the atmosphere and are influenced by the exact pulling power of Earth's gravity. Stick us somewhere with too little pressure and we explode. Too much, and we implode. Gravity too strong? We can't move. Gravity too weak? Our muscles waste away.

Then there's the temperature and the breathable atmosphere. Human beings have to maintain a core body temperature of around 98.6°F to stay healthy. At just a few degrees higher or lower, we die of hypothermia (being too cold) or hyperthermia (being too hot). We also need to breathe oxygen—but if the air contains too little or too much, we die of hypoxia or oxygen toxicity.

Wow! I didn't realize what a bunch of weenies we were. So we need good air, gravity, and nice weather?

Right.

So how does the Moon measure up? Or Mars?

Not well, I'm afraid. You wouldn't want to hold a party on either. The Moon has no atmosphere at all, and we can only describe the atmosphere on Mars as "bad" (about 96% poisonous carbon dioxide). On top of that, Mars has one-third of the surface gravity of Earth, and temperatures range from 68°F down to a lethal −220°F. As for the Moon, that has one-sixth the surface gravity of Earth, and temperatures go from an insanely hot 266°F down to an insanely cold −274°F. Not exactly what you'd call prime vacation destinations.

What about other planets? Can't we just find one the same as Earth and go there?

We're already working on the first part. The search for Earth-like planets has been on for some time now. NASA's *Kepler* satellite will orbit the Sun for four years as it studies distant stars for signs of Earthlike planets nearby. This will be followed by the Terrestrial Planet Finder—a huge telescope built in space for a similar purpose. There's a good chance we'll find an Earthlike planet with one of these. Getting there, though, may be the more difficult part.

Why's that? Would it be too far away?

Basically, yes. Even the closest planet outside our solar system would take hundreds of years to get to, so unless we develop much, much faster spacecraft, we're stranded for the time being. If we were desperate to leave Earth, we could reach other planets within our solar system, like Mars, and try to build ourselves an artificial Earthlike environment. Perhaps the first few pioneers could build a survival station or dome, to be enlarged by later arrivals. But even that wouldn't be easy. Aside from the distance (Mars is over 48 million miles away and it'd take nine months to get there), you'd have a major problem with the weight of the spacecraft. Just loading up the people plus enough fuel and food and water supplies for the round trip would make the craft too heavy to launch. And that's without the building materials for the dome.

So we couldn't even make it to Mars?

Well, we might be able to get around this by building the craft in space, or using the water and carbon dioxide on Mars to make methane fuel for the return trip. But the main thing is—if it's so much effort to get there and make it livable, then is it really worth going at all? The same goes for other, more distant planets—only more so, as they'd be even harder to get to.

What do you think?

I'd say right now it isn't worth it. But if conditions on Earth were to change—like if it became too overpopulated, too polluted, or too hot to live on—then maybe it would. Hopefully by then we'll have figured out the trans-portation problem too, so it won't take months or years to get there. But for now, at least, I think I'll stay at home. Besides—there's football on TV tonight . . .

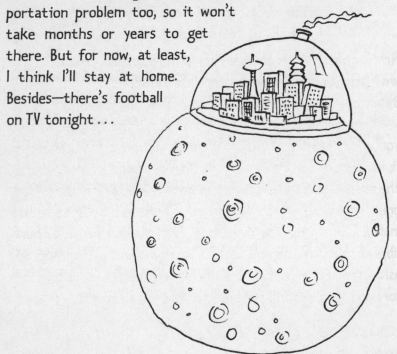

What will school be like?*

No teachers? No classes? Maybe you'll go to a building, but students will study their own unique subjects. Maybe you won't go at all. One thing's for certain—it'll be different.

No teachers?! That sounds excellent! But how would we learn stuff with no teachers around?

By yourself, using online libraries, guides, and experiences.

In traditional classrooms, you wait for the teacher to tell you what he or she knows, write it down, and try to remember it in case you're tested later. In the classrooms of the future, the teachers won't be keepers of the knowledge any more—for one thing, there will be too much for any one teacher to know. Instead, you'll be able to search for information in virtual libraries on any subject you can imagine. And if you need to ask a specific question, the world's greatest virtual professors and teachers will be there to help you answer it.

---

* The vision of future schools and education used in this question borrows heavily from Roger C. Shanks's essay "Are We Getting Smarter?" in the compilation *The Next 50 Years*, John Brockman (Ed.), Phoenix Books, 2002.

But how would we know what to study for tests and exams?
That's where a teacher, guide, or learning assistant would come in. They might give you learning goals or set challenges for you to accomplish. But they wouldn't ask you questions and expect you to chirp up the correct answers. Instead, they would simply set the theme or topic, and you would be expected to ask the questions and find the answers by yourself. Besides all that, tests and exams would be different too.

How?
They would be much less about questions and answers, and more about understanding problems, describing experiences, and meeting challenges. Or there might be no exams at all. You might graduate from a class by collecting virtual merit badges for the experiences you've had, instead.

So if you could study on your own, using the Internet for info, what would be the point in going to school at all?
Maybe you wouldn't. Maybe you'd have the option to stay at home. But I think most people would go—because you get more out of going to school than simply learning about stuff.

Like what?
Even if you studied by yourself, you still might need guidance and advice from the teacher at stages along the way. Then there's meeting friends, playing sports, and joining clubs. Of course, you could do all these things online too, but you'd miss out on all the fun that comes with meeting people face to face and doing physical, active things in the real world. The

point is that in the end you'd go to school because you wanted to, rather than because you have to.

All right! I'm all for that. So if you went, would the people there be the same? Just the learning would be different?
Not necessarily. It might not be like school as you know it—where people are divided into groups that all study the same subject at the same time. Instead, a class might contain thirty or forty individuals all studying their own subject, at their own pace. In fact, the only thing they might have in common is that they live in the same area. So it could be more like a community school, where you go to school with everyone in your neighborhood.

Sounds cool. But would that really work—all that "experience instead of being taught" stuff?
Many experts in learning and education believe so. And they're backed up by some of the greatest minds in history. Galileo, the famous Italian astronomer, physicist, and philosopher, once said, "You cannot teach a man anything; you can only help him discover it within himself." (Which I'm sure he would have been happy to apply to both boys and girls, were he here today.)

The also-quite-clever German scientist Albert Einstein followed this a couple of hundred years later with his advice: "The only source of knowledge is experience."

I'm in. When can I start?
Right away. No matter where you go to school, how you learn can still be up to you. Just dig in and enjoy yourself.

Index